Sprachkrimis Englisch

Frightened to Death

Oliver Astley
Jennifer Pickett
Anne Ellsworth

Genehmigte Sonderausgabe

Baierbrunner Str. 27
81379 München

Umschlaggestaltung: Andrea Pfeifer, Kommunikation+Design
Umschlagabbildung: www.fotolia.com, Sandra Cunningham

ISBN 978-3-8174-8933-6
381748933/1

Vorwort

Krimispannung auf Englisch!

Die in diesem Band enthaltenen drei Sprachkrimis helfen Ihnen dabei, Ihre Englischkenntnisse ganz nebenbei zu verbessern und bereits Gelerntes zu festigen. Auf unterhaltsame Weise kombinieren die Krimis Lesevergnügen mit sinnvollem Sprachtraining. Abwechslungsreiche Übungen ergänzen die einzelnen Geschichten und machen so das Lernen spannend und effektiv. Die dazu passenden Lösungen finden Sie am Ende des Buches.
Durch Vokabelboxen auf jeder Seite können Sie unbekanntes Vokabular gleich mit der Übersetzung auf einen Blick erfassen und neue Wörter prägen sich Ihnen leichter ein.
Ihren Lernerfolg können Sie mithilfe des ausführlichen Abschlusstests überprüfen und so das Sprachtraining abrunden. Zusätzlich bieten Ihnen nützliche Infokästen Wissenswertes zu Themengebieten wie Landeskunde, Sprache und Grammatik.

Viel Spaß beim spannenden Sprachtraining!

Inhalt

Frightened to Death 5
Death in the Woods 47
Dressed to Die 81
Abschlusstest 140
Lösungen 142

Frightened to Death

Die ältere Dame Catherine Wallis stirbt unter geheimnisvollen Umständen in ihrem Häuschen. Wer könnte ein Motiv haben, sie zu töten? Oder sind hier gar übernatürliche Kräfte im Spiel?

Death in the Woods

Der Unternehmer George Morris wird tot im Wald aufgefunden – offensichtlich kaltblütig ermordet. Wer hatte einen Grund, den Mann umzubringen? Spielen Waffengeschäfte eine Rolle?

Dressed to Die

In London treibt ein Serienkiller sein Unwesen. Bereits zwei Opfer wurden tot am Ufer der Themse gefunden. Als der Killer einen dritten Mord ankündigt, ist Spürsinn gefragt – schafft Scotland Yard es, ein weiteres Verbrechen zu verhindern?

Frightened to Death

Oliver Astley

1 A Fright in the Night

Everyone knew everything about everyone in Llanprid, a charming old village in the middle of Wales. Many of the residents were related, most were friendly towards each other, and those who were neither friends nor relatives loved gossiping about each other.

The same families had lived in the same houses for at least three generations, and young lovers often strengthened the close-knit community by getting married. Few people decided to move away forever. Those who did were usually the black sheep of the family.

One example was Peter Wallis, the adopted son of Catherine Wallis. Everyone knew he was not really a Wallis, but nobody knew his real surname. Even the other children in Llanprid had not accepted the strange, tall boy who had arrived in their village when he was nine years old. He had always been an outsider, and he was happy to leave the place almost ten years later when he began studying law at university. Since then, he had never looked back.

Peter did not stay in close contact with anyone in the village apart from Catherine. After all, she was the nearest thing he had to family. And Catherine, who was very proud of her son, never tired of telling her neighbours about his achievements. This made it difficult for the other residents of Llanprid to forget about Peter Wallis, that unusually quiet person who always dressed in black.

Now in his mid-thirties, Peter was a successful lawyer in Cardiff. Although he did not have the time to visit Catherine very often, he

residents *pl*	Einwohner
to gossip	tratschen
close-knit community	enge Gemeinschaft
to tire of doing sth.	müde werden, etw. zu tun
achievements *pl*	Leistungen

to keep in touch	in Verbindung bleiben
shaky	zittrig
to get hold of sb.	jmd. erreichen
to put the kettle on	Wasser aufsetzen
only child	Einzelkind

kept in touch on the telephone, and he sent a postcard whenever he went on holiday.

At the start of their conversation one early Sunday evening, Peter noticed that his mother sounded very upset.

"Oh, Peter!" she began, "I'm so glad I could reach you."

Catherine did not usually call on Sundays because that was the day Peter rang her; his mother's turn was on Wednesdays. They always spoke after her favourite television programme ended at 9 p.m. This was something that had simply become a tradition.

"You know I always have my mobile with me," he answered. "I was going to call you later. Is everything all right, Mum?"

"No, not really," she replied in a shaky voice. "It's not all right at all. There were some horrible noises coming from upstairs earlier, and they started again a few moments ago... I can't get hold of any of the neighbours. I don't know what to do!"

"Try to relax, Mum," said Peter calmly. "Put the kettle on and tell me what you mean."

Peter could remember growing up in that old cottage. He had been an only child, but there had been lots of spiders and mice to play with. Some of the neighbours' cats often came round as well, either to eat the food he put out in the back garden for them or to hunt fresh mice for themselves. It meant that there were always funny noises coming from somewhere. But his mother was certain that she could hear a human voice this time, and that someone was laughing and calling her name.

"It sounded like Cyril!" she told him.

to think straight	klar denken
divorce	Scheidung
↯ to jump out of one's skin	erschreckt hochfahren
heart failure	Herzversagen
to sigh	seufzen

"I'm sure there's nobody else in the house," he replied. "How could there be? You always lock the doors, don't you?"

Catherine agreed, and before the kettle had even started whistling she was beginning to sound a little more relaxed. Talking to Peter helped her to think straight, and he was right about one thing: living alone since the divorce had made her very nervous.

"I only have to hear the doorbell ring and I almost jump out of my skin," she joked. "My poor heart will be the death of me."

A long time ago, the Wallises had been one of the largest families in Llanprid. Nature was not on their side, though: many of Catherine's relatives had died of heart failure before they reached the age of forty.

"That's how I lost both my mother and your uncle," she remembered aloud and sighed.

Exercise 1: Lesen Sie weiter und ergänzen Sie den Text mit dem passenden Wort!

(front doorbell neighbours surprise)

Suddenly the 1. ____________ rang and Catherine jumped up in 2. ____________. "Oh! Just a minute, dear," she said. "There's someone at the 3. ____________ door."

"Do you really think you should answer it?" asked Peter.

"Yes, it'll be one of the 4. ____________. I left a message with Mary asking her to come round. I'll call you later."

cane	Spazierstock
to startle sb.	jmd. erschrecken
china	Porzellan
to shuffle	schlurfen
shape	Gestalt, Form

Peter paused again and finally agreed, "Okay, Mum."

"Goodbye, dear!" she said and hung up.

Catherine picked up her cane and began walking towards the front door. On her way, she was startled by a loud knocking from the other side of the house. It sounded as if there was somebody at the back door. Was it possible? She'd just been sitting there in the kitchen.

"Who's there?" she called.

There was no answer from either side of the house, but again a knocking came from the back door. Three loud bangs filled the small cottage. The knocking was so strong that Catherine could hear the china plates next to the sink dancing from side to side. Her heart began to race.

Maybe Peter was right, she thought. She shouldn't open the door to anyone, just in case.

"Who is it?" she shouted again nervously.

"Hello, Cathy! Is everything all right?" asked a familiar voice from the other side of the back door.

Finally! There was only one person who called her "Cathy". She turned around and shuffled along the corridor and back into the kitchen. A shape moved behind the glass. Catherine felt much safer knowing that someone had come to keep her company.

The kettle was whistling loudly now; she would make them both a nice cup of tea.

After turning the key in the lock with a shaky hand, she opened the door.

Exercise 2: Übersetzen Sie die Wendungen aus dem Text!

1. Ist alles in Ordnung? ______________________
2. nur für alle Fälle ______________________
3. ein bekannte Stimme ______________________
4. die Porzellanteller ______________________

"Thank heavens you're here," she began. "It's been such a..."

She fell silent when she saw the face looking back at her. It was not the familiar[i] face she was expecting, but a white, **expressionless** mask. Her eyes opened wide and her heart began to beat even faster. The voice that came from inside was as dark and frightening as the empty, black eyes staring straight at her.

"Such a scary evening?" it **mocked**.

False Friends

familiar ≠ familiär
familiar = bekannt, vertraut
personal, informal = familiär

Catherine dropped her cane and put both hands over her mouth. Her heart seemed to stop beating in her **chest**. Her skin was suddenly covered in a cold **sweat**. She tried to step back into the kitchen, but the dark figure moved too quickly.

All the old woman could do was panic and look around helplessly for someone to save her. She tried to scream, but it was **pointless**; she had no breath to scream. Moments later, Catherine Wallis'

expressionless	ausdruckslos
to mock	spotten
chest	Brust
sweat	Schweiß
pointless	zwecklos

lifeless body was lying on the cold kitchen floor. Her dead eyes stared at the ceiling in horror. On top of the cooker, the steaming kettle was jumping and screaming as if it had **witnessed** the **entire** scene.

to witness	miterleben, Zeuge sein von
entire	ganz, gesamt

Exercise 3: Welcher Satz ist korrekt? Kreuzen Sie an!

1. a) ❐ Peter's Catherines adopted son.
   b) ❐ Peter's Catherine's adopted son.

2. a) ❐ He helped her thinking straight.
   b) ❐ He helped her to think straight.

3. a) ❐ There was a loud knocking at the door.
   b) ❐ It knocked loudly at the door.

4. a) ❐ Catherine was death on the floor.
   b) ❐ Catherine was dead on the floor.

2 The Man in Black

Raven Close was a typical road for an old village. It ran along the edge of John Bidderscum's farm, so one side was **lined with** trees and a very thick **hedge**. On the other side there was a row of houses, each of which had a small front garden. In the summer these gardens were full of colourful plants and flowers, but now, by late October, the ground was covered with brown leaves.

Catherine Wallis lived next door to a woman whose back garden looked like a jungle. Her name was Mary Giles, and – as she always used to tell the young postman – she could not look after the house because of her bad leg.

The postman was one of the few people who **regularly** spoke to Miss Giles. She was a lonely pensioner who had argued with every family on Raven Close over the years. The only real friends she had left were her cats – and Cathe-rine, who liked the old woman's strong personality and lovingly called her "the old **battle-axe**".

lined with	gesäumt von
hedge	Hecke
regularly	regelmäßig
ϟ **battle-axe**	Dragoner, (alter) Drachen
to distract	ablenken

When Miss Giles stepped outside to call in Theodor, one of her cats, the whistling coming from her neighbour's house made her stop and listen. Seconds later, her attention was suddenly **dis-tracted** by something moving in the long grass in her garden. She thought it was her missing cat.

"Theodor? The-o-dor! Dinner!" she shouted.

A dark figure that was at least twenty times larger than Theodor stood up on two legs, ran up the garden and disappeared through a hole in Miss Giles' fence. She **gasped** and hurried back into her house, forgetting all about the whistling.

When ten minutes later Theodor had still not scratched at the door to be let in, the old woman opened her door to call him again. Immediately she heard the whistling noise again and **wondered** what it could be.

to gasp	keuchen, nach Luft schnappen
to wonder	sich fragen
to hobble	hinken
to give out	*hier:* von sich geben
flashing	blinkend, aufleuchtend
paramedic	Rettungssanitäter

Miss Giles **hobbled** across to the hedge that separated her garden from Catherine's and noticed that her neighbour's back door was wide open. That was strange, she thought. Suddenly she saw a hand lying in the doorway and **gave out** a horrified scream.

Exercise 4: Lesen Sie weiter und unterstreichen Sie die Gegenteile der angegebenen Wörter!
(departed in the middle bored before behind nodding)

The ambulance arrived first on Raven Close and parked on the side of the road. The **flashing** blue lights brought several interested faces to windows and doors. The neighbours wanted to see what was going on at the Wallis cottage.

Shortly afterwards, a police car parked in front of the same house and two officers in uniform stepped out of the vehicle. One of the **paramedics** walked up to them, shaking his head, and invited them both inside.

Within ten minutes the front door opened again, and the two officers left the cottage. They put on their hats and made their way next door to the woman who had called the ambulance.

plump	pummelig
to blink	blinzeln
superior	Vorgesetzter
to wipe	abwischen

Some of the villagers recognized Inspector Davies, the tall, thin man with grey hair who knocked on Miss Giles' door. Nobody knew the plump officer who was with him, though.

"I knew something bad was going to happen to that poor woman," Miss Giles said mysteriously as soon as she opened the door. "I can see these things."

Inspector Davies blinked at the woman, who paused to look at him over her thick, black glasses before she continued.

"I can," she said knowingly. "I read Catherine's tea leaves only last week. There was a clear picture of a cross at the bottom of the cup, as well as a fork, a heart and the letter J."

"What does that mean?" the young officer asked her politely.

"It means nothing at all," her superior answered brusquely. "Can Sergeant Jones and I come inside to talk to you, Miss Giles?"

"You can come in," she answered, "but wipe your shoes first."

It was almost 9 p.m. when the police began interviewing Miss Giles, and they were still listening to her long stories over half an hour later.

"Please let's concentrate on the facts," said Inspector Davies in a tired voice. "Can you describe the person you saw in your garden just before you called the ambulance?"

"It was a big man, that's all I can tell you for certain," she replied.

tartly	bissig, mit scharfer Zunge
to knit	stricken

"Oh, and he was wearing black. That much was clear when he got up and ran away. My outside light was on."

"Are you sure it was a man, Miss Giles?" asked Sergeant Jones.

"Absolutely. He was at least six feet tall, and there are no women around here like that," she said a little tartly.

Inspector Davies smiled slightly and asked his next question: "Can you think of anyone who may have wanted to hurt Mrs Wallis?"

The old woman gave a sharp laugh.

"Let me tell you one thing, Inspector," she answered. "Catherine Wallis was a sweet, kind lady. She was harmless, and everyone loved her – apart from that Cyril, of course."

The inspector looked at the woman, expecting further details, but she picked up some wool and began to knit.

Exercise 5: Beantworten Sie die Fragen zum Text!

1. Who called the ambulance?

   ____

2. How is the person in the garden described?

   ____

3. Which of the two police officers is thinner?

   ____

4. What did Miss Giles do to see Catherine's future?

   ____

"Miss Giles," Inspector Davies said calmly, "we need to know everything you know about the deceased that could be important. We cannot be certain yet what, or who, caused her death."

the deceased	der/die Verstorbene
to mutter	murmeln, nuscheln
to grumble	murren, brummen
unshaven	unrasiert
flatly	ausdruckslos
to be lost for words	sprachlos sein

"Then you should go and speak to Cyril Rogers yourself," she muttered. "The less I talk about that man the better." (i)

Sergeant Jones looked at her notes. Miss Giles had already told them a few basic details about Catherine Wallis, including her family history. She had mentioned Cyril Rogers' name a couple of times before: he was Mrs Wallis' ex-husband.

A couple of hours later that same evening, the police finally found somebody in at Cyril's house, but they were not given a warm welcome.

> **the ... the ...**
> Vergleichssätze nach dem Muster **je ... desto ...** werden im Englischen mit **the** + Komparativ the + Komparativ wiedergegeben, z. B.: **the bigger the better.** Es wird also die erste Steigerungsform des Adjektives verwendet. Die Wortstellung ist dabei die des normalen Aussagesatzes.

"What time do you call this?" grumbled a very tall, unshaven man.

He obviously had not noticed the uniform of the young woman standing in front of him. His cheeks and nose were bright red, and his breath smelled strongly of beer.

"Mr Rogers? I'm sorry to disturb you," said Sergeant Jones politely, "but I'm afraid we have some bad news about your ex-wife."

"Cathy? I know she's dead," he replied flatly. "Everybody was talking about it at the pub tonight. Is that all you wanted to tell me?"

Inspector Davies and Sergeant Jones were lost for words. Cyril Rogers did not appear to be at all upset about Catherine's death.

to swallow	schlucken
suspicious	verdächtig
to divorce	sich scheiden lassen

"It's very tragic, of course... so sudden," he added when he saw that the two were studying his face very closely.

"We're still trying to find out exactly what happened," explained the inspector. "Is it okay if we ask you a few questions?"

Cyril suddenly looked a little worried. He swallowed nervously and asked the question that was on his mind: "You don't think someone killed her, do you?"

"It's too soon to say whether the death is suspicious or not. However, a witness saw someone dressed in black near Mrs Wallis' house earlier this evening, and we would like to find out who that was," Inspector Davies explained. Cyril did not respond. His eyes were like glass.

"Were you at the pub all evening, Mr Rogers?"

"Of course! I stayed there after the rugby with all the boys."

Cyril Rogers was not an athletic man, and at the age of fifty-six he was not a boy either. But the Welsh rugby team had played against Ireland in the afternoon, and most of the fans in Llanprid went to watch such matches on the television screen at The Red Dragon.

"You should speak to the Stevens family if you haven't done that yet," he said before Inspector Davies could ask his next question. "Their young boy James is nothing but trouble."

Sergeant Jones made a note of the Stevens' address and told Cyril that they would definitely visit every family in the area.

"Is it right that you divorced Mrs Wallis only a month ago, Mr Rogers?" Inspector Davies asked.

Cyril moved his eyes from the sergeant's notebook to the inspector and gave him an angry look.

"It became official in September, yes," he replied shortly. "But we've been separated for over two years."
"And you left her for another woman, if I understand correctly," the inspector continued.
"Look, if you want to accuse me of something, just say it!" Cyril snapped.
"Nobody is accusing anyone of anything, Mr Rogers," Inspector Davies replied in a calm voice. "We're just finding out everything we can about your ex-wife."
Sergeant Jones watched the two men exchange looks. They were staring at each other as if they were trying to read each other's minds during a game of chess.

to accuse sb. of sth.	jmd. etw. vorwerfen
to snap	*hier:* blaffen
to read sb.'s mind	jds. Gedanken lesen
chess	Schach
pacemaker	Herzschrittmacher

"I left her for another woman, but the two of us are not together any more. Catherine was quite ill," said Cyril slowly. "I'm very sorry that she's dead, but it's not a big surprise."
He repeated what Inspector Davies had already learnt about Mrs Wallis: she had needed a pacemaker and had taken tablets because of a weak heart.
"Did you see each other very often?" the inspector continued.
"Yes, sure," Cyril said. "You can't hide from anyone in a village this small, but we had nothing to say to each other most of the time."
A woman's voice from upstairs called Cyril's name.
"Look, can we talk about this tomorrow?" he asked. "Thanks for coming round, but I don't think I can help you."
Sergeant Jones was about to say something when Inspector Davies put his hand on her arm.

to slam	zuschlagen

"That's fine, Mr Rogers," he said pleasantly. "You have a good night and we'll continue our questions here or at the station tomorrow. Here's my card. Just give me a call if there's anything you want to tell me in the morning."

Cyril **slammed** the door shut without even saying goodnight and hurried upstairs to the voice that was still calling him.

Exercise 6: Ordnen Sie den Wörtern die passende Definition zu!

1. ☐ to hang up	a) to find boring
2. ☐ to tire of	b) to visit
3. ☐ to come round	c) to contact
4. ☐ to get hold of	d) to end a telephone call

3 The Grim Reaper

On the following morning, a large crowd of people had gathered again outside the Wallis cottage. Sergeant Jones arrived and looked at the house. The front wall was a strange pink colour, which she had not noticed the night before. It seemed as if half the residents of Llanprid were there, although all they could see was a lot of parked cars and some tape around the house. The **forensics** team was busy at work inside.

the Grim Reaper	der Sensenmann
forensics	Spurensicherung
accidentally	versehentlich, unbeabsichtigt
to compete	wetteifern

It was the most exciting thing that had happened in the village since John Bidderscum, the man who owned the farm across the road, **accidentally** drove his tractor into Catherine Wallis' front garden. Everybody was gossiping about the night before and Cyril Rogers' many reasons for wanting to get rid of his ex-wife.

Sergeant Jones was among the crowd. She had tried to find people in their houses, but most of them were either at work or standing at the end of Raven Close. There was a lot of information to collect, so she was hectically taking notes as the villagers **competed** with each other to speak.

"Cyril hated Catherine," said one voice, "and they were always arguing with each other."

"That's right," another person agreed. "I remember a fight they had only last month. Very nasty, it was. I'm sure Cyril said he would kill Catherine if she came anywhere near his house again..."

Suddenly everyone stopped talking and turned their heads towards Cyril Rogers' house down the road. The front door opened and a very tall woman stepped outside. She closed the door, looked at the crowd, paused for a moment, then crossed the road in the opposite direction.

disapproving	missbilligend
investigation	Ermittlung, Untersuchung
mortuary	Leichenhalle
next of kin	nächster Angehöriger

"That's Vivienne Gray," whispered one of the old ladies. "She must be Cyril's new partner. She's half his age!"

"Isn't she with Bidderscum's youngest, the postman?"

"Just look at her!" said another woman in a **disapproving** voice. "That woman's all legs and no heart. How can anyone wear such a tiny skirt on a cold and windy day, I ask you?"

Sergeant Jones saw Vivienne Gray look back over her shoulder at the group of people. This was someone she definitely wanted to talk to, she thought.

"I'll be back in a few minutes, ladies," she said and ran after the woman.

Exercise 7: Welches Wort ist das „schwarze Schaf"? Unterstreichen Sie das nicht in die Reihe passende Wort!

1. planned intentionally accidentally knowingly
2. heart lungs brain skeleton
3. unlock close slam shut
4. flat expressionless unemotional excited

Meanwhile, Inspector Davies was organizing the **investigation** at the police station in the nearby town of Welshpool. Catherine Wallis' body was at the **mortuary**. Peter Wallis, the **next of kin**, was

pointy	spitz
injury	Verletzung
forced entry	gewaltsames Eindringen
to frown	die Stirn runzeln
weeds	Unkraut
evidence	Beweis

coming to Llanprid; the police in Cardiff had contacted him on Sunday night.

In over twenty years with the police, the inspector had not worked on many murder cases. Such serious crimes were not common in the countryside, but things did not look good on Raven Close.

Inspector Davies was sitting at his desk eating an egg sandwich when the forensics expert entered his office. She was a very serious woman with short, black hair and a pointy nose. Her face always reminded the inspector of a crow.

"Ah, hello Jenny," he said. "Have you brought me some news about Catherine Wallis?"

"There's very little to tell you, Stewart," she answered. "There's no sign of injury on the body and there was definitely no forced entry into the house. The kitchen's clean; it looks like nobody had been in there apart from the deceased."

Inspector Davies took another bite from his sandwich.

"What about the person Miss Giles saw in her garden?" he asked with a full mouth.

Jenny frowned and pulled out some photographs from a brown envelope.

"There's nothing obvious yet," she said. "But you've seen what the team has to look at, haven't you? There are dead leaves everywhere, and the weeds in the neighbour's garden have grown very tall. It will be some time before they finish collecting evidence."

The inspector sighed and asked when the autopsy was going to take place. It was impossible to investigate a death without knowing for sure whether murder was involved. And at this point he had no weapon, no motive, and no real **suspect**.

suspect	Verdächtiger
apparently	angeblich, anscheinend
trace	Spur

At that moment the telephone rang. It was Sergeant Jones; she had finished interviewing the residents of Raven Close. Jenny pointed at her watch to say that she was busy.

"Tomorrow," she whispered and walked away.

He nodded and listened to what Sergeant Jones had to report: most of the families had been at home or at The Red Dragon on Sunday evening, she explained, and nobody apart from Miss Giles had seen a suspicious person dressed in black. Mr and Mrs Stevens were **apparently** on holiday, and there was no **trace** of their son James.

Exercise 8: Setzen Sie die Verben in der korrekten Zeitform ein!

(read investigate search read tell work)

1. Right now they ________________ the garden for evidence.
2. She will be tired if she ________________ all night.
3. The sergeant ________________ many murders before.
4. I ______________________ this book for over two weeks now.
5. She ____________________ the newspaper when he came in.
6. I ______________________ her about the news this morning.

"There is one thing, though, sir," Sergeant Jones said after the inspector sighed again.

incident	Vorfall, Ereignis
to offend sb.	jmd. beleidigen
hanging basket	Blumenampel
a blazing row	ein furchtbarer Streit
pansy	Stiefmütterchen

"Oh? What's that, then?" he asked, suddenly interested.

"Well, it's about Cyril Rogers. He told us last night that he had spent the entire evening at the pub with his friends, but that wasn't true."

"Not true, you say?" the inspector repeated.

"No, sir. Well, he was there all right, but he left for around an hour between 7:30 and 8:30. And that's not all..."

"Go on, Jones," Inspector Davies said after swallowing the last mouthful of his egg sandwich. "I'm listening."

"People have seen him and Mrs Wallis arguing recently. They didn't speak for a while because their lawyers were writing a lot of letters, but there have been a couple of incidents since the divorce."

"What do you mean by 'incidents'?"

"Well, it's a bit childish, really. Mr Rogers' new girlfriend offended Mrs Wallis in the post office last month, and so she cut off all the (i) heads of the flowers in his hanging baskets later that day. There was a blazing row when he caught her."

All the ... bezeichnet eine eingeschränkte, bestimmte Menge, all ohne Artikel wird dagegen in allgemeinen Aussagen verwendet, z. B. All women like flowers.

"I see," said the inspector flatly but with a smile on his face. "And do you think that someone's life is worth a few pansies?"

"Of course not, sir," she replied. "But Cyril's words were very clear. He said, 'I'll kill you if you come anywhere near my house again.'"

"Well, he does seem to be an aggressive man," he agreed.

Inspector Davies was about to ask Sergeant Jones to bring Cyril Rogers to the station for questioning when the receptionist came around the corner with that very person beside him.

urgently	dringend
in charge of	zuständig für
to contain	beinhalten
threat	Drohung, Bedrohung
scythe	Sense

"Oh, speak of the devil! I'll call you back later, Jones," he said and raised his eyebrows at the two men who had just entered the room.

"Gentlemen?"

"A Mr Rogers from Llanprid to see you, Inspector," announced the receptionist. "He said he urgently needs to speak to the person in charge of the Catherine Wallis case."

Cyril Rogers walked up to Inspector Davies' desk and dropped a plastic bag on the table. It contained what looked like a large playing card.

"What do you make of that, then?" he asked without saying hello.

The inspector slowly looked at both sides of the card.

"Where did you find this?" he asked.

"Someone put it through my letterbox this morning," Cyril answered. "It's clearly a threat!"

The card showed a skeleton dressed in a black robe and holding a long scythe; at the top was a number in Roman numerals.

"Oh dear," Inspector Davies said, his eyes fixed on Cyril's, "number thirteen. That's unlucky for some, isn't it?"

It had been a long time since the inspector had seen a tarot card. This one was the most famous one, though. And almost everyone

solemn	düster
to return	zurückkehren
nosy	neugierig
smart	*hier:* schick

knows the solemn picture of Death – or the Grim Reaper, as he is also known.

"Did you receive a note or anything else with this, Mr Rogers?" the inspector continued.

"No, nothing at all. Why?"

"Well, obviously it would help us identify where the card came from. Do you have any idea who might have a reason to threaten you?"

Cyril looked alarmed. "No! Anyone could have delivered it," he snapped.

"I see. Well, never mind. We'll have the card examined and see what we can find."

"Is that all you have to say?" Cyril demanded in a loud voice. "Isn't it obvious that somebody wants me dead?"

Inspector Davies scratched the back of his head and told the man that he was welcome to stay at the station for a few hours if he felt that his life was in danger. In any case, they would have something important to discuss as soon as Sergeant Jones returned from the village.

Later that day, an expensive car turned into Raven Close and parked opposite the Wallis cottage. Nosy faces watched the driver getting out of the vehicle from their living room windows. It was a tall man in a smart, black suit. Most people recognized him immediately when he stood up and turned around. They had not seen him for several years, but there was no question about it: it was Peter Wallis.

Exercise 9: Lesen Sie weiter und bilden Sie sinnvolle Wörter aus dem Buchstabenchaos!

Peter looked at the faces in the windows from the other side of the road.

A few heads were (1. dingond) ________________ at him in **sympathy**.

"Come here, you poor thing!" a (2. eicov) ____________ suddenly said behind him.

As Peter turned, Miss Giles put her thin arms around him. She had just left her house and was still (3. ginrycar) ________________ her knitting. The long needles **poked** him in the back.

The (4. scorefins) ______________ team was still busy examining his mother's cottage and the two gardens, so Peter went next door to speak with his old (5. roughbien) ________________.

"Make yourself (6. crobfmotlea) ________________, dear," Miss Giles said as they passed the kitchen door. "I'll put the (7. etketl) ____________________ on and we can have a good chat."

The **peculiar** smell of Miss Giles' house made Peter feel like he was a child again. He saw that the sofas were covered in cat hair

sympathy	Mitgefühl
to poke	stechen
peculiar	seltsam

and decided to sit down at the living room table. Whenever he looked out of the window, he saw four people walking around in white suits.

Theodor, one of the oldest cats, was sitting between two black and white photographs on the windowsill and staring at a big spider.

windowsill	Fensterbank
wrinkly	runzlig
to read sb.'s palm	jmd. aus der Hand lesen
bad luck	Pech
deck	*hier:* Kartenspiel

"You still have a lovely house, Miss Giles," he lied as she carried a tray of black tea into the living room.

The old woman was not interested in talking about herself. Instead, she kept saying how shocked she was about Catherine's death and told Peter all about the questions that the police had asked.

"You have a difficult road ahead," she said and pressed her cold, wrinkly hand against his.

Before he realized what she was doing, Miss Giles had put on her thick glasses and was reading his palm.

"But I see a happy future for you, eventually," she explained. "You will have a long and successful life and many children to share it with."

Peter smiled politely. He had heard the same story several years ago when Miss Giles had last tried to tell his fortune.

"You're not going to get out your tarot cards, too, are you?" he joked.

Miss Giles took off her glasses and put them down on the table.

"Of course not, dear," she smiled. "There's a card missing, and it's bad luck to use an incomplete deck."

Exercise 10: Übersetzen Sie und enträtseln Sie das Lösungswort!

1. Stiefmütterchen ☐ _ _ _ _
2. Menschenmenge _ _ ☐ _ _
3. Fensterbrett _ _ _ _ _ _ _ _ ☐ _
4. Verletzung ☐ _ _ _ _ _
5. vorwerfen _ _ ☐ _ _ _
6. beleidigen _ _ _ ☐ _ _

Lösung: ☐☐☐☐☐☐

4 Ghosts

Cyril Rogers left the police station with a red face. He had changed his alibi for Sunday evening to include the hour or so he had spent with Vivienne Gray. He could not remember the exact times.

Inspector Davies remained sceptical.

"The two of them could be working together," he suggested to Sergeant Jones, who was adding the report from the forensics department to the case file.

"They both fit Miss Giles' description," she added. "After all, all she saw was a tall person dressed in black. We have no idea if it was really a man or a woman."

case file	Fallakte
will	Testament

The inspector muttered something about the bad eyesight of old people and that she had probably imagined the whole thing.

"What about their motive, though?" he continued.

"I'm not sure, sir, but I've been thinking about that. Mrs Wallis had no children with Mr Rogers, and she changed her name two years ago, a long time before the divorce was final. She probably left everything to her adopted son."

"I see," said the inspector. "I'll see what I can find out about her will."

"What about the death threat that Mr Rogers received?" Sergeant Jones asked. "Do you think someone could have a reason to kill both him and Mrs Wallis?"

"I wouldn't be surprised if he was inventing the whole thing to make himself appear innocent," the inspector said. "He didn't tell us about his arguments with Mrs Wallis, and he was very quick to accuse James Stevens. We should definitely **observe** that man very closely. In that way, we'll either be **protecting** him, or we might catch him."

to observe	beobachten
to protect	(be)schützen
to turn sth. down	etw. ablehnen
ϟ Long time, no see!	Lange nicht gesehen!
witch	Hexe

Back in Llanprid, Peter Wallis was searching for an excuse to **turn down** a third cup of tea when somebody knocked loudly at the front door.

"I'll get it," he said to Miss Giles.

Peter walked along the hallway, taking care not to step on the cats as he went.

Exercise 11: Lesen Sie weiter und bringen Sie die folgenden Sätze in die richtige Reihenfolge!

a) "Terribly sorry to hear about your poor mum," he said. "Very sad news, it was. Everyone in the village is thinking of you."

b) "Hello there," said the man in a cheerful voice. "**Long time, no see!**"

c) "Who's there?" Miss Giles called from the other side of the house. She sounded like an old **witch** when she shouted so loudly.

d) He opened the door and did not recognize the man on the other side.

1	2	3	4

to sort out	*hier:* in Ordnung bringen
to bother sb.	*hier:* jmd. beschäftigen

"It's John!" the man shouted back and smiled nervously at Peter, who obviously had no idea who John was.

"You've really grown up, Peter! You're almost as tall as me now."

Peter couldn't think of anything to say but showed the visitor into the living room, where he offered him some tea from the pot.

"I thought you were that Cyril Rogers," said Miss Giles. "You sound just like him, you know."

"Oh yes, people often tell us both that."

It became clear through the conversation of the two villagers that the man was John Bidderscum, the farmer who owned the field on the other side of Raven Close.

"Anyway, Mary, you're probably wondering why I came over," John announced, suddenly changing the subject.

Peter saw the farmer look out of the window for the third time. He seemed distracted by the forensics team.

"I've been telling you for a long time that I would come and sort out your garden, so I thought I would do it today before the weather turns bad. It will be winter soon."

Miss Giles was very happy to hear this, but there was an obvious problem that Peter was quick to mention: the police were still at work in her back garden.

"I can see that!" replied John. "I can start around the front, though, and you can let me know when the police have finished whatever it is they need to do. I've brought everything I need."

John Bidderscum went back outside and began unloading his van. Moments later, Peter asked the old woman a question that had been bothering him.

to exclaim	ausrufen
to suppose	annehmen, vermuten
aerial	Antenne

"Why's he being so friendly? Everyone here hates the Bidderscums, don't they?"
"No, dear!" she **exclaimed**. "What makes you think that? They're a very nice family, especially John and his wife."
"I don't know... something my mum told me once, I **suppose**."
"Oh, well – yes. Your poor mother didn't like him very much, but the Wallises and the Bidderscums have always fought like cat and dog. John was here yesterday as well, you know. He promised he would repair the television **aerial** on my roof. He looked a bit tired, but he said he didn't mind. I'm always telling his son how difficult it is for me to look after the place. Do you remember Gareth, their youngest? He's the village postman now."
Peter had stopped listening to Miss Giles. He remembered that the police in Cardiff had told him to call an Inspector Davies when he arrived in Llanprid: he had to arrange a time to look around his mother's cottage and see whether anything had been stolen.

Exercise 12: Übersetzen Sie folgende Sätze!

1. Wir lassen den Brief morgen untersuchen.

   ____

2. Gestern Abend wollte er ihr Gesellschaft leisten.

   ____

3. Soll ich jetzt das Wasser aufsetzen?

   ____

tool	Werkzeug
to intend	beabsichtigen
to make the most of sth.	das Beste machen aus
valuable	wertvoll
haunted castle	Spukschloss
cobweb	Spinnennetz
to put the final touches to sth.	etw. den letzten Schliff geben

It was the last day of October, and heavy rain in the late afternoon made John stop working in the front garden just as the sky began to grow dark. That was very atmospheric for Hallowe'en, he thought.

He put his tools into his van and told Miss Giles that he was going to buy some food in town and asked if she needed anything.

Further down the road, James Stevens was preparing the biggest party of his life. His parents were still on holiday in Egypt, and he intended to make the most of their large house. Everyone at the local high school knew that he was throwing a Hallowe'en party. Those with an invitation had planned their costumes weeks ago.

James had had a very busy day. First he had locked away anything valuable that his friends could break or steal, then he and his two best friends had spent hours making the house look like a haunted castle. Candles were already burning on the windowsills, and all of the rooms contained spooky decorations and cobwebs. There was also a skeleton that the boys had stolen from the biology room at school.

Once the work was done, they began putting the final touches to their costumes before the first guests arrived.

"Have you invited the neighbours?" asked Count Dracula.

James smiled innocently. "Of course I have! Something tells me they won't come, though."

"That's a shame!" laughed Frankenstein's monster. "This party's going to be wild! All those pensioners would be a good catch."

James sniggered and picked up his plastic scythe.
"Yeah, they would," he agreed. "But even Death needs to have a night off and relax sometimes!"
He placed a white mask over his face and pulled his black hood over the top of his head.

to snigger	(hämisch) kichern
hood	Kapuze
unmarked car	Zivilfahrzeug (der Polizei)
to sob	schluchzen
unmistakable	unverwechselbar

Later that evening, Sergeant Jones and one of her junior colleagues were observing Cyril Rogers. They were sitting in an unmarked car outside The Red Dragon. It was raining heavily.
The suspect and his girlfriend had entered the pub arm in arm less than an hour ago. The whole village knew by now that he and Vivienne Gray were together, so they were being much less discreet about their relationship.
Suddenly, the door opened and Cyril ran around the side of the building. He sat down on a step and began to sob, his face buried in his arms.

Das zusammengesetzte Adverb **somewhat** (etwas, ein wenig) wird analog zu **somehow** oder **sometimes** verwendet, um einen unbestimmten Grad zu bezeichnen.

Seconds later, Sergeant Jones' attention moved from Cyril Rogers to her colleague's camera, which was pointed at a tall figure leaving the pub. The long legs were unmistakable: Vivienne Gray was marching away in the opposite direction.
"Oh dear, Tom!" the sergeant said, somewhat[i] amused. "It looks like there's trouble in paradise. I wonder if their alibi will last as long as their relationship?"

screeching brakes	quietschende Bremsen
to pretend	so tun, als ob; vorgeben
passer-by	Passant
to run sb. over	jmd. überfahren

At that moment the sound of screeching brakes filled the air. A car had come to an abrupt stop just outside The Red Dragon where Vivienne had been crossing the road.

"You crazy idiot!" shouted an angry woman. "You could have killed me!"

Cyril recognized Vivienne's voice and got up to see what was going on. Sergeant Jones sent Tom after him to investigate. Tom pretended to be an ordinary passer-by.

"What happened here?" he asked. "Is everyone all right?"

Exercise 13: Ergänzen Sie das jeweilige Adverb und Substantiv!

1. heavy ____________________ ____________________
2. suspicious ____________________ ____________________
3. helpless ____________________ ____________________
4. innocent ____________________ ____________________

"No!" shouted Vivienne in a shaky voice. "He tried to hit me!"

"What a load of nonsense," replied the driver shortly.

The driver was the man whom Tom had seen working in Miss Giles' garden that afternoon. He listened to the two arguing while Cyril silently watched on with an open mouth. Vivienne had been going out with one of the man's sons, Gareth, and she was accusing him of trying to run her over like a dog.

5 Revenge

The first morning of November was the start of a busy day for Davies. The autopsy results for Catherine Wallis arrived before noon, and it was confirmed that she had **died of natural causes**.

"Heart failure," he told Sergeant Jones without expression.

"But we know there's more to it than that, sir!" Seargant Jones **objected**.

"Yes, and our young lawyer from Cardiff knows that, too," he replied. "Let's try to stick to the facts here."

The inspector scratched his head and began to summarize his conversation with the son.

to die of natural causes	eines natürlichen Todes sterben
to object	einwenden
executor	Testamentsvollstrecker, Nachlassverwalter

"Peter is the **executor** of his mother's will. Both he and Cyril knew that Catherine had left everything to Peter, even though Cyril had to give a lot to Catherine after the divorce. Are you with me so far?"

"Yes, I see," the sergeant said. "What else did he have to tell you?"

"Now then, on Sunday evening he stopped talking to his mother when somebody visited her. She told him that a neighbour was at the door and hung up."

"A neighbour?" Sergeant Jones asked in surprise.

"Yes. According to Peter, Catherine had left a message on Miss Giles' answering machine; she had also spoken to a woman at Mr Rogers' house."

"Vivienne? But Catherine couldn't stand her or Cyril!"

"I know," the inspector replied. "She sounded very frightened on the phone. She said she'd heard Cyril upstairs at around 6 p.m."

fibre	Faser
to recreate	nachbilden
to rummage around	herumwühlen
muddy puddle	Schlammpfütze
encouragingly	ermutigend

"But he was at the pub. That makes no sense!" Sergeant Jones said.

"Well, those are the facts. It's our job to make sense of them."

The inspector showed her the case file.

"The forensics team found some black fibres in Miss Giles' garden where our mystery person climbed over the hedge," he said.

"I don't know if that will help us unless we find someone wearing torn clothes," she smiled.

"Well, quite. They also discovered a number of footprints. The rain has destroyed most of the evidence, but they're working to recreate an entire footprint."

"What kind of footprint are we looking at?"

Inspector Davies rummaged around on his desk and pulled out a brown envelope from a pile of papers. Inside there were three photographs showing what appeared to be muddy puddles and a length of measuring tape.

"Apparently our man wears size twelve or thirteen shoes. That's all we know."

"Pretty big! We know we're looking for a man, then," said Sergeant Jones encouragingly. "That's something, at least."

Their first visit that afternoon was to Cyril Rogers' house. He was as polite as ever when he opened the door.

"What the hell do you want this time?" he snapped.

Cyril found it amusing that the police wanted to look at his shoes, and he did not understand why they were disappointed when he

to settle differences	Differenzen beilegen
severed	abgetrennt
deaf	taub

showed them that he wore a size eight.

"Never mind his shoes, Inspector," said a tart voice. "What are you going to do about that madman up the road who tried to kill me?"

It was Vivienne Gray, dressed in a black bathrobe. Apparently she and Cyril had **settled** their **differences**, thought Sergeant Jones.

"Ah, Miss Gray," the inspector replied, "I believe you forgot to tell my colleague that you'd spoken to Mrs Wallis shortly before her death."

"That's right, I forgot!" she said. "Well, it was a very short call."

Inspector Davies frowned but asked her to describe yesterday's incident with John Bidderscum outside the pub. Sergeant Jones had not yet mentioned it because of all the other developments at the station that morning. He listened politely at first, but he soon tired of the village politics. After all, nobody had been injured.

Exercise 14: Lesen Sie weiter und unterstreichen Sie die richtige Variante!

The pair next stopped at a house that had **severed** heads 1. (in / on) the windowsills. Cyril had 2. (said / told) the police that James Stevens was definitely back in the village: only a **deaf** person 3. (would have / could have) ignored the party those kids were having last night, he 4. (said / had said) angrily.

sheepishly	einfältig
to flick through	durchblättern
neatly	ordentlich, sauber
laundry basket	Wäschekorb
to approach	sich nähern

The teenager who opened the door smiled sheepishly at the police.

While Sergeant Jones was speaking, the inspector looked him over from head to toe. The boy was a giant and his feet were huge.

"Can you tell us where you were between 7 p.m. and 9 p.m. on Sunday evening?" she asked.

"Erm...," James Stevens said after a pause, "oh yeah, I was bowling in Welshpool."

The sergeant noted down some details and said they would be in touch.

"We'll have to check the boy's alibi before we question him," Inspector Davies said as they walked up the road to Miss Giles' house. "But I'm more interested in John Bidderscum now. Have you already spoken to him? He sounds as loud and aggressive as Cyril Rogers!"

Sergeant Jones flicked through her black book, stopped at a page with a lot of neatly written notes and smiled.

"Oh yes, he was very pleasant, actually. He gave me a lot of details, but none of them seemed very important. Let's see... on Sunday he returned from a fishing trip in the evening and went straight to bed."

At the top of the hill, they could see Miss Giles' front garden. It was very tidy, although someone had apparently emptied their laundry basket onto the grass. As they approached, the inspector saw that the colourful pile was in fact a number of cats lying on the lawn.

to crackle	knacken, knistern
rockery	Steingarten

The old lady watched the police arrive from her living room window and invited them in. She seemed to be rather nervous.

"Let me come to the point, Miss Giles," said the inspector the minute she began with her usual small talk. "Mrs Wallis told her son that she left you a message on Sunday. Do you remember that?"

"A message? No, I've not received one for days, and it's impossible to ignore the flashing red light. I'm not blind, you know!"

At that moment her television crackled and the picture disappeared.

"Oh, dear!" the old woman cried. "How am I going to watch my favourite soaps now? It was only two days ago that John fixed the aerial."

Inspector Davies frowned and asked how often the man visited.

"Oh, he's been an angel ever since that accident with the tractor," she said. "Do you know he ruined Catherine's lovely garden and destroyed my rockery? He was ever so [i] upset about it all."

The inspector was trying to make sense of the weekend's events.

"Did you leave Mr Bidderscum alone in your house on Sunday?" he asked.

"No," she said, thinking. "Well, only when I was looking for Theodor."

There was a short pause in which both police officers exchanged a meaningful look. It was long enough to miss a phone call.

"Do you mind if I have a look upstairs, Miss Giles?" the inspector suddenly asked. "Sergeant Jones will keep you company here."

> Mit der typisch britischen Wendung **ever so** wird in der Umgangssprache eine Aussage verstärkt. Z. B.: ever so many – sehr viele, ever so slightly – ein ganz klein wenig

Exercise 15: Lesen Sie weiter und setzen Sie die fehlenden Wörter ein!

The 1. s____________ smiled **reassuringly** when 2. h____________ superior disappeared up the 3. s____________. She asked Miss Giles whether Mr Bidderscum also used to visit Mrs Wallis from time to 4. t____________. The old lady laughed.

"Now there's a story!" she said happily. "The Bidderscums and the Wallises don't get along very well at all. It must be in the blood. There was a **family feud** for generations when there were more of them. They were always fighting or competing to **outdo** each other, and dear old Catherine was very proud of her family's history."

Miss Giles made some tea and began talking about the Wallis family, many of whom had died at a young age. Inspector Davies then returned and whispered something into his colleague's ear.

reassuringly	beruhigend
family feud	Familienfehde
to outdo sb.	jmd. übertreffen
shade	*hier:* Farbton, Schattierung

"Think very carefully," began Sergeant Jones. "Did Mrs Wallis do anything recently that might have upset John Bidderscum?"

There was a short pause.

"Well," began Miss Giles, "there was that whole business with the cottage, I suppose. Catherine had the front of her house painted last week. You must have noticed that it's a funny **shade** of pink."

"Why would that have upset Mr Bidderscum?" the inspector asked impatiently.

"That's obvious," she said in her tart voice. "The Wallises have lived in that house for only two or three generations. The Bidderscums used to live there before that, you see – some of them, anyway. It was Robert Bidderscum who built the cottage back in the 1870s..."

to change hands	den Besitzer wechseln
rightfully	rechtmäßig
ominously	unheilvoll
to light up	*hier:* aufleuchten, strahlen
furious	sehr wütend
to be off	*hier:* weggehen
bin	Mülleimer

Miss Giles picked up a photograph from the windowsill.

"That's him there with my grandfather," she explained.

"So the cottage changed hands at some point?" asked the sergeant.

Miss Giles nodded and told them that Catherine's mother had moved into the house with a Bidderscum after he married for a second time. It was a long and complicated story.

"In short, some of the older Bidderscums might feel that the house is still rightfully theirs, if I understand it correctly," the inspector said.

"Just imagine seeing 'your' house painted a strange pink colour one day," added Sergeant Jones ominously.

Miss Giles' face lit up.

"Oh, he was furious! Now you mention it, I remember him making quite a few comments. I won't repeat words like that, though."

Inspector Davies smiled innocently and thanked the old woman.

"You've been very helpful," he said, "but we must be off now."

Miss Giles watched the police leave, then she shuffled across the living room to the table. She picked up her incomplete deck of tarot cards and threw them into the bin.

"I thought I was in trouble then, Theodor!" she said to the cat. "At least I gave that Cyril Rogers a little fright!"

Exercise 16: Ergänzen Sie das richtige Fragewort!

1. ______________________ about your promise to help me?
2. ______________________ about telling me everything from the start?
3. ______________________ does he come to visit you?
4. ______________________ do you like your tea, Inspector?

John Bidderscum was singing when the police found him feeding the pigs on his farm. He was standing up to his ankles in mud.
"Please don't talk to me about Vivienne Gray," he sighed when the inspector asked him to explain what had happened on the previous night. "I'm quite busy, and I've got no time for that **slut**."
Inspector Davies was surprised by the man's language.
"Sorry," the farmer continued, "but she broke my young **lad's** heart."
"Maybe we could talk about your visits to Mary Giles, then," the inspector said.
John smiled and explained that he tried to be a good neighbour.
"And you wanted to keep an eye on what the police were doing."
The man turned and looked at the inspector, who had picked up one of the large, dirty **trainers** that were on the wall next to the **pigsty**.
"Miss Giles has already destroyed your alibi for Sunday," Inspector

ϟ slut	Schlampe
ϟ lad	Bursche, Junge
trainers *pl*	*hier:* Turnschuhe
pigsty	Schweinestall

to freeze	*hier:* erstarren
loft	Dachboden

Davies said. "I wonder if this shoe matches the footprints we found." John froze for a moment and replied, "I don't know what you mean."

The inspector continued to explain that he knew that Mr Bidderscum had fixed Miss Giles' aerial on Sunday, and that it was possible to enter Mrs Wallis' loft from her neighbour's house.

"Peter Wallis told us that his mother heard a voice up there. She didn't know who it was, but I think we might have the answer.

The farmer looked very serious and walked out of the pigsty.

"I didn't mean to kill her!" he objected. "Sure, I wanted to frighten her a little, but I'd forgotten that the old girl had such a weak heart."

"We'll see about that," said Inspector Davies ominously. "I think we should go to the station now and talk this over in detail, don't you?"

A few days later, Miss Giles was reading the local newspaper when she saw the headline about Catherine Wallis and dropped her spoon. It read: "Llanprid Pensioner Scared to Death."

"It all makes sense to me, Theodor," she told her cat. "The heart, the farmer's fork, the letter J for John... I saw it all in her tea leaves."

Death in the Woods

Jennifer Pickett

1 Murder

Stephen slipped silently into the house. His heart was thumping violently in his chest. He made his way up the darkened stairs to his room. With every step he was terrified that he would be caught. He lay fully clothed on his bed, his body tense and his eyes moving wildly around the room. He was exhausted but sleep wouldn't come. The hours crawled slowly past.

"Dead, dead, dead."

The word pounded relentlessly in his mind. From downstairs he could hear the voices of his mother and stepfather talking as they made breakfast. His mother's quiet voice was soon lost under the louder, more aggressive voice of Arthur, his step-dad. He was complaining about the traffic on the Clifton Suspension Bridge. Stephen buried his head under his pillow.

"What am I going to do?"

He bit his lip to stop himself from crying out in fear. He had never been so scared in his life. Every time he shut his eyes he could see the whole horrible scene playing out in front of him. He knew it was only a question of time before the police caught up with him.

to slip	*hier:* hineinschleichen
to thump	*hier:* pochen
tense	angespannt
to crawl	kriechen
to pound	hämmern
relentlessly	schonungslos
suspension bridge	Hängebrücke
stubble	Bartstoppeln

Detective Inspector Charles Billington and Sergeant Daniel Fox looked at the busy area in front of them. DI Billington rubbed his hands over his tired face. Stubble prickled against his skin where he hadn't shaved that morning. He had put on fresh clothes that morning but they already looked **creased**. At forty-five he was getting too old for these early mornings.

Exercise 1: Lesen Sie weiter und unterstreichen Sie alle sieben Adjektive!

His young sergeant, however, looked rested and seemed full of energy. Danny's thick black hair was slightly messy, but other than that he looked as if he had just come from a relaxing afternoon watching the cricket!

The usual peace of these woods on the hills over Bristol had been **disturbed**. The area was now alive with activity. The black and yellow police tape fluttered in the breeze. Even though it was still early, a small crowd had gathered. Detective Inspector Billington **sighed** as he recognized the reporter from the local newspaper. The serious-looking constable on duty was doing a good job of making sure that no one crossed the tape into the **crime scene** behind, but the detective knew it wouldn't be long before the questions started.

"Right, Danny, let's **get this over with**."

He led his sergeant past the constable at the tape and into the **clearing** in the centre of the woods. He nodded at the **forensics** team at work.

"Morning, Andrew, what have you got for me, then?"

Andrew Cavendish, the forensics team leader sat back on his heels and looked up at him.

to crease	zerknittern
to disturb	stören
to sigh	seufzen
crime scene	Tatort
ϟ to get sth. over with	etw. hinter sich bringen
clearing	Lichtung
forensics	Kriminaltechnik

"The body is of a man about fifty years old. Cause of death is likely to be a shotgun blast to the chest."

The body was lying on its back with its arms out to the sides. The man was obviously dead. The blood from the huge gun shot wound in his chest had stopped flowing a long time ago. It had soaked into the man's shirt and coat and into the leaves below his body.

shotgun blast	Schuss aus einer Flinte
to soak	*hier:* durchsickern
post mortem	Autopsie
to survey	begutachten
gun club	Schützenverein
↯ inside job	Werk von Insidern
lack of progress	mangelnder Fortschritt

"It looks like he has been dead for several hours. Time of death would be in the early hours of this morning," said Andrew before adding, "but we won't know for certain until the post mortem."

DI Billington stood back from the corpse and surveyed the scene. Sergeant Fox came to stand by his side. He took one look at the body and said, "I know him, sir."

"You do?"

"Yes, sir. It's George Morris, a local landowner and gun club owner. I met him a few weeks ago. He had come to the station to talk to Detective Singh, the officer in charge of his case. A number of rare, expensive guns had been stolen from his club, sir. Detective Singh thought it may have been an 'inside job'. Mr Morris had come to complain about the lack of progress."

The DI looked thoughtfully at the body. "George Morris. Hmm, I've heard of him."

"I wonder what he was doing in the woods in the middle of the night, sir?" said Danny. "It's such an isolated spot."

"I don't know, Sergeant, but look around you. The undergrowth has been disturbed in a wide area around the body. There was a struggle."
"Whatever George Morris found in this clearing last night, I don't think he was expecting it."

Exercise 2: Bringen Sie die Buchstaben in die richtige Reihenfolge!

1. It's such an (teioslad) ____________ spot.
2. There was a (ggrutsel) ____________.
3. George had come to (inoacpml) ____________ about the lack of progress.
4. The (grurwnotedh) ____________ has been disturbed.

The group of policemen and women huddled together near the entrance to the woods. It was a cold morning and the officers were stamping their feet to keep warm. The police vans that were parked at the side of the road provided a bit of shelter from the wind. Detective Inspector Billington had taken care to move his officers far enough away from any members of the public so that he could talk without being overheard.
"Okay, let's start at the beginning. Who found the victim?"
A young, tired-looking officer stepped out of the crowd.
"Constable Marsh, sir," he said introducing himself. "I found the body."

undergrowth	Unterholz
shelter	Schutz, Unterschlupf
to overhear	zufällig hören
victim	Opfer

overweight	Übergewicht
to explore	*hier:* durchsuchen
torch	Taschenlampe
grateful	dankbar
clue	Hinweis

DI Billington nodded for him to continue.

"The control centre received a phone call at ten past three this morning. The caller said that a man had been shot in these woods. The control centre sent Constable Roberts and I to investigate."

Constable Roberts, an overweight officer with dark circles under his eyes, nodded in agreement.

DI ist die Abkürzung für **Detective Inspector** und entspricht ungefähr dem deutschen Begriff Hauptkommissar.

"Was the caller here when you arrived?"

"No, sir," continued Marsh. "The call was anonymous. The caller wouldn't give his name. He hung up when he was asked again. It was still dark when we arrived, so it took us a while to find the body. We called for an ambulance and we have been here ever since."

Constable Marsh thought about their unpleasant experience in the middle of the night. The woods had been very cold and dark when they arrived. The two policemen had explored the woods with only torches to help them. They had begun to think the call was a fake when they finally found George Morris' body. Constable Marsh had nearly fallen over him in the dark.

"Well done, son," said the DI. "Go home now and get some sleep."

The two Constables headed gratefully back to their car. DI Billington addressed the rest of his officers.

"Sergeant Nicholls, I want you to get onto the control centre. They record every call that comes in. I want a copy of that recording. It's our first clue. Someone was here when George Morris was shot or found him not long afterwards. Who was that person and why didn't they stay around?"

A number of the officers **shrugged**. People who wouldn't give their names to the emergency services usually had something to hide. It wouldn't be an easy job to find their mystery caller.

to shrug	die Schulternzucken
donation	Spende
ϟ to be all over sth.	*hier:* sich über etw. hermachen
to remind	daran erinnern

"Sergeant Fox will divide you into groups. I want officers to visit every house nearby to see if anyone saw or heard anything and I want officers searching the rest of the woods for clues. We already have people on their way to tell George Morris' family the news. Sergeant Fox and I will head to the victim's gun club. George Morris was shot. That will be a good place to start."

Exercise 3: Fügen Sie an den richtigen Stellen die Apostrophe ein.

1. Stephens boots.
2. The callers name.
3. Stephens mothers voice.
4. The two constables torches.
5. George Morris family.

Detective Inspector Billington had one last thought for his officers. "George Morris was a well-respected member of Bristol's community. He made generous **donations** to the local school and to other groups in Bristol. People know who he is. The press is going to **be all over** this one. I don't need to **remind** you not to speak to

investigation	Untersuchung
curious	neugierig
to pretend	so tun als ob
to scan	*hier:* absuchen

anyone who is not directly involved in the investigation. We need to do this correctly and catch this killer quickly."

As Detective Inspector Billington and Sergeant Fox walked back to their car, Danny felt as if they were being watched. Curious to see if he was right, he paused and pretended to retie his shoe laces while he scanned the trees. There was no one to be seen. Seconds later, as he shut the car door, he thought he heard a dog bark.

2 A Suspect!

The officers who visited George Morris' family had found it an upsetting experience. They hadn't learnt anything new that would help their investigation. George seemed to have been a well-loved man who helped out his community.

As they parked outside the gun club, Detective Billington and Sergeant Fox knew that they needed to find some clues.

"A gun was involved in the murder and guns have recently been stolen from the club. We can't rule out a connection to the gun club," said the DI.

upsetting	verstörend
flustered	aufgeregt
to burst into tears	in Tränen ausbrechen
gamekeeper	Wildhüter
groundsman	Platzwart

Danny nodded in agreement and led his boss into the club's reception area. Florence, the elderly secretary, was very flustered to see the police waiting at her desk. The news of George's death hadn't reached the club yet, and when Detective Billington explained the reason for their visit Florence burst into tears.

"I'm sorry to have to tell you this news but we need to ask you some questions about Mr Morris and about the recent break-in at the club."

Once Florence had calmed down slightly she suggested that they speak to Thomas Cruickshank, the club's gamekeeper and groundsman.

"He will be able to help you more than I can. Thomas has worked here for years and has been friends with George for even longer. I can't imagine what this will do to him."

The thought of Thomas' reaction to the news was enough to start Florence crying again, and it was a few minutes before the policemen could leave her in order to find the gamekeeper.

Exercise 4: Welche Aussagen sind korrekt? Markieren Sie mit richtig ✔ oder falsch – !

1. Thomas told Florence that George had died. ❐
2. Guns had recently been stolen from the club. ❐
3. No one liked George Morris. ❐
4. Thomas had worked at the gun club for years. ❐

"Thomas Cruickshank?"

The man in the shabby brown overcoat was kneeling by a flowerbed pulling up weeds. He adjusted his cap and looked up when he heard his name. His dirty brown dog had been sleeping at his side but stood up growling as the policemen approached.

"I'm Detective Inspector Billington and this is Sergeant Fox. We'd like to ask you some questions about George Morris. I assume you have heard the news?" asked Inspector Billington.

weeds *pl*	Unkraut
ϟ Aye	Ja
acquaintance	Bekanntschaft

"Aye," said Thomas sadly. "His son rang me shortly after the police had left their house. How can I help you?"

Thomas was able to tell the policemen about the layout of the gun club, George's usual routines and acquaintances. They were left with a much better idea of the dead man.

"What can you tell us about the recent robbery?" asked Sergeant Fox. "Did you see anything or anyone suspicious in the area in the days before the guns were stolen?"
"Not really. I spoke to the police at the time. I told them that I had seen some youths hanging around a couple of evenings before the break-in. They were drinking beer and kicking a football around but nothing more sinister. I didn't see them that night."
Sergeant Fox continued to ask questions about the break-in as Detective Billington reached into his pocket to answer his ringing phone. Constable Walker, the female officer on the other end of the line, sounded slightly breathless with excitement.
"Sir, we've found something."

robbery	Raub
suspicious	verdächtig
sinister	*hier:* schlimm
breathless	atemlos
to shatter	*hier:* (zer)stören
bordering	angrenzend

Danny steered the car through the winding lanes near the gun club. Both men were silent with their own thoughts. The peace was shattered by the shrill ring of the DI's mobile phone.
"Detective Inspector Billington speaking."
Danny waited patiently while his boss finished his call.
"That was Sergeant Nicholls calling from the control centre. He has a copy of the anonymous call to the emergency services last night. Our mystery caller sounded like a teenager or young man although Nicholls couldn't be sure. He did say the caller sounded extremely frightened."
Detective Billington and Sergeant Fox found Constable Walker standing on the doorstep of a small cottage bordering the woods where the body of George Morris was found.

Exercise 5: Lesen Sie weiter und unterstreichen Sie die richtige Variante!

She 1. (listened / was listening) to a **bent** old lady who was talking **animatedly**. Her glasses were perched on the end of her nose. The old lady 2. (was holding / held) Constable Walker's arm with one hand and a walking stick in the other. The constable 3. (looked / was looking) as if she 4. (was feeling / felt) a bit trapped. The look of **relief** on her face 5. (was / has been) obvious when she saw the two policemen walk up the garden path to join her. After she 6. (was introducing / had introduced) them, Constable Walker turned to the elderly lady.

"Mrs..."

"Just call me Peggy."

"Peggy, could you please tell the Detective what you have just told me."

"Well, young man, as I was just telling the constable here, I suffer badly from arthritis. Terrible it is! It keeps me awake a lot of the time. I hope you never suffer from it young man. The things I could tell you..."

Constable Walker rolled her eyes at the good-looking Sergeant Fox. He **winked** at her and she **blushed**. He could imagine how hard it must have been to listen politely to the old lady's **ramblings**.

bent	gebeugt
animatedly	angeregt
relief	Erleichterung
to wink	zuzwinkern
to blush	erröten
ramblings *pl*	Gefasel, Geschwafel

painkiller	Schmerzmittel
↯ shifty	durchtrieben
↯ to be up to no good	nichts Gutes vorhaben
to trespass	widerrechtlich betreten
pheasant	Fasan

"Yes, as I was saying, last night I was getting a drink of water so I could take my painkillers. You can see the woods from my kitchen window. It must have been, oh, about three o'clock this morning. I remember because my cat was awake too and she always wakes up around three..."

"Peggy," reminded Constable Walker, "please tell Detective Billington what you heard."

"A gun shot!" she paused for dramatic effect. "Then I saw that boy running from the woods."

"Which boy?" asked the DI.

"Stephen McDougal. A shifty boy from the next street. He hangs around on his own a lot. He has no friends. He's obviously up to no good!"

Danny Fox was taking notes.

"And," continued Peggy, "I know that George Morris recently had words with Stephen's parents about his trespassing in the woods. Thomas the gamekeeper had seen him there several times and thought the boy might be stealing pheasants[i]."

In Großbritannien spielt die Jagd nach wie vor eine große Rolle. Besonders Fasane sind ein beliebtes Beutetier.

"What?" Peggy peered up at Constable Walker. "Speak up, dear."

Constable Walker spoke very loudly and slowly. "Tell Detective Billington what you heard."

"When, dear?"

Constable Walker rolled her eyes in frustration.

"Last night, Peggy. What did you hear?"

Exercise 6: Finden Sie das passende Verb und setzen Sie es in die korrekte Zeitform!

(call exchange do not look be)

After Constable Walker had taken Peggy back into her house to sit down, Detective Billington and Sergeant Fox 1. ______________ looks. The old woman really had been rambling. It was also quite obvious that she was a bit deaf and that her eyesight wasn't brilliant. How good a **witness** 2. ______________ she? Just then they were 3. ______________ by a young woman in the front garden of the house next door.

"Er, excuse me officers. I 4. ______________ mean to overhear but could I have a word?"

The policemen walked round the hedge separating them to join the woman in her garden. She was young, blonde and 5. ______________ tired.

"Hi, I'm Gemma. I was awake at around three, too. I have a new baby and she doesn't let me get a lot of sleep! I heard the gun shot and when I looked out of my window, I saw a man running from the woods. It was too dark for me to see who it was, though."

witness	Zeugin

"This must be the same person Peggy saw!" exclaimed Sergeant Fox.

"Possibly," said Gemma slowly. "I heard you talking to Peggy. I should warn you, she's a lovely lady but once she gets an idea in her head then you can't change her mind.

DI Billington smiled sympathetically.

"She has told me that she has seen Stephen McDougal going in and out of the woods at odd times," continued Gemma. "She may have got this confused with last night. Also, recently she has decided that Stephen is a troublemaker. If you believe everything she says, then he is some sort of criminal mastermind or terrorist!"

to change one's mind	sich etw. anders überlegen
sympathetic	mitfühlend
odd	ungewöhnlich, seltsam
ϟ troublemaker	Unruhestifter
loner	Einzelgänger
pushchair	Kinderwagen

"What do you think?" asked DI Billington.

"He seems harmless to me. A bit of a loner but he has never done anything to make me worry. He helped me with my baby's pushchair once and he was very polite."

Just then the sound of a baby's cry came from the house. Gemma sighed.

"Sorry, I have to go."

The policemen thanked her for her help and as they returned to their car, Detective Inspector Billington turned to his sergeant.

"Danny, we need to speak to this Stephen McDougal. He's currently our only suspect. Suspicious behaviour, history of trespassing, one witness and we know it was a young man who made the call to the emergency services. Let's go."

3 Unexpected Visitors

Stephen McDougal lived in a small cottage with his parents. There was nothing interesting or remarkable about it. There was nothing to say this might be the home of their murderer. A short, red-faced man opened the door to them.

"What has the stupid boy done now?" he said angrily when he saw the policemen.

Sergeant Fox was a bit shocked at the man's reaction.

"Er, nothing that we know of, sir. We would just like to talk to Stephen McDougal. We understand he lives here. Is he your son?"

The man snorted.

"No, thankfully. My name is Arthur Evans. Stephen is my stepson. My wife June is his mother."

Arthur gestured to a small mousy woman the officers could see looking nervously over the man's shoulder.

"Please come in," she stammered. "Stephen is in the back room."

DI Billington and Sergeant Fox followed June down the hall. At the living room door she turned and looked timidly at Detective Billington.

"Please don't upset him, Officers. He's a good boy and was very unsettled after George Morris came to the house and accused him of trespassing. Did you know?"

"No Ma'am, we hadn't realized that Mr Morris came here. How long ago did this happen?"

"Well, it was a few weeks ago now. George was very nice about it, really, but quite stern. Stephen

remarkable	auffallend, bemerkenswert
to snort	schnauben
mousy	farblos
to stammer	stottern
timid	schüchtern
unsettled	unruhig
to accuse of	beschuldigen
stern	ernst

was quiet and distant for days afterwards. He wouldn't talk to us about it."

George's mother didn't seem to realize that she wasn't helping her son's situation. Stephen got to his feet when the officers entered the room. He was a slim boy of about sixteen, wearing jeans and a dark T-shirt. His brown hair was a little too long and fell forwards over his face.

Exercise 7: Welcher Satz ist korrekt? Kreuzen Sie an!

1. a) ❐ "What has the stupid boy done now?"
   b) ❐ "What did the stupid boy do now?"

2. a) ❐ Nothing that we now of, sir.
   b) ❐ Nothing that we know of, sir.

3. a) ❐ Stephen has been quiet and distant for days afterwards.
   b) ❐ Stephen was quiet and distant for days afterwards.

4. a) ❐ He got to his feet when the officers entered the room.
   b) ❐ He got too his feet when the officers entered the room.

"What's going on, Mum?"

"It's nothing to worry about love," June said gently. "The officers just want to ask you some questions about George Morris. You know they found his body in the woods this morning."

gently	sanft, zärtlich

at the mention	bei der Erwähnung
to glare at sb./sth.	etw./jmd. wütend anstarren
agitated	aufgeregt

Stephen's face went white **at the mention** of George Morris.

"We also want to talk to you about some guns that have been stolen from the club."

"What?" said Stephen shocked. "I don't know anything about stolen guns!"

"Of course you don't," snorted Arthur.

Detective Inspector Billington **glared at** him.

"Stephen, we just want some information [i]. No one is accusing you of anything at the moment."

"I haven't done anything!" cried Stephen in frustration.

"Calm down, son," said Danny. "We've got a witness who said that she saw you running out of the woods on the night of George's murder."

"I wasn't there! It wasn't me. They must have made a mistake!"

"Okay, then tell us exactly where you were at around 3 a.m. this morning."

Stephen's mum spoke up.

"He was in bed. Weren't you, Stephen?"

"Yes, of course," Stephen replied.

But he wouldn't meet the policemen's eyes.

"What are you hiding, son?" asked Detective Billington gently.

"Nothing!" shouted Stephen, suddenly very **agitated**. "I wasn't there. I don't know anything about George Morris!"

Sergeant Fox stepped towards Stephen to try to calm him down. As he put his hand on the young man's shoulder, Stephen suddenly gave him a big push.

Information wird im Englischen grundsätzlich nur im Singular verwendet. Im Deutschen hingegen können wir den Begriff auch im Plural verwenden.

"No!" he cried out.

Stephen spun around and fled out of the back door of the cottage. It took Danny Fox a second to get his balance and then he ran after him. He **caught a glimpse** of Stephen's T-shirt as he disappeared into the woods at the back of the **property**.

Exercise 8: Welches Wort ist das „schwarze Schaf"? Unterstreichen Sie!

1. mention say hear speak
2. suspicious sinister shifty sympathetic
3. detective witness sergeant inspector
4. frustrated agitated calm animated
5. tidy clean chaotic washed
6. full nothing empty unfilled

"He's a good **lad** officers, honestly! He wouldn't hurt anyone," protested June.

"Running away from the police never looks good," replied Detective Billington.

"How are we supposed to know what the boy is doing when he is out of the cottage?" **muttered** Stephen's stepdad.

"Shut up, Arthur," **hissed** June.

Arthur looked at her shocked. He obviously wasn't used to her answering back.

to catch a glimpse	einen Blick erhaschen
property	Grundstück
ϟ lad	Bursche, Junge
to mutter	grummeln
to hiss	zischen

Minutes later Danny arrived back in the cottage alone and shook his head at his **superior**.

"I've lost him."

Stephen ran as fast as he could. Once he was certain he had lost his **pursuer**, he **crept** silently back towards the cottage. He lay on his stomach in the bushes at the edge of the woods. He needed to know what was happening and he knew the policemen had to leave eventually.

superior	Vorgesetzter
pursuer	Verfolger
to creep	schleichen, kriechen
patience	Geduld
to reward	belohnen
patrol car	Streifenwagen
to occur to sb.	jmd. ein fallen

Stephen's **patience** was **rewarded** when the cottage door opened. He could see the two officers talking to his mother on the doorstep. Their voices floated back to him.

"Your son is hiding something, Mrs Evans. Please call us as soon as he reappears. Don't make us come looking for him."

He couldn't hear his mother's reply as she shut the door firmly behind them.

As the policemen got into their car, DI Billington gave his orders.

"Call the station, Danny. I want Stephen McDougal's description given to every **patrol car** in the area. If anyone sees him, they should stop him immediately. I want to talk to that young man. Right, it's been a long day. Let's finish for tonight."

Very early the next morning, the DI and sergeant went back to the murder scene. The detective liked to visit the scene of crime again to see if anything new would **occur to him**. The sun hadn't yet risen fully and the clearing was still quite dark and full of shadows.

"What are we missing, Danny?" he asked softly.

Exercise 9: Ergänzen Sie die Aussagen und enträtseln Sie das Lösungswort!

1. Stephen hid in the ☐ _ _ _ _
2. Stephen moved _ ☐ _ _ _ _ _ _ _ , without making a noise.
3. Stephen and his parents lived in a _ _ ☐ _ _ _ _
4. Stephen is Arthur's _ _ _ _ _ _ _ ☐
5. Sergeant Fox is a _ _ _ _ _ _ ☐ _ _ _
6. DI Billington is Danny's ☐ _ _ _ _ _ _ _ _ _ _
7. Sergeant Fox ☐ _ _ _ _ his head.

Lösung: ☐ ☐ ☐ ☐ ☐ ☐ ☐

"I don't know, sir. Everyone who knew George Morris seems to have liked him. We haven't been able to find any enemies who might **hold a grudge**. And then there is Stephen. He is definitely hiding something but he seems scared to me. You saw his room, sir, all those nature books. He is a loner who prefers nature to people."

"You're right. And with a **bully** like Arthur Evans for a stepdad, I'm not surprised," DI Billington commented.

to hold a grudge	einen Groll hegen
bully	Tyrann

"Exactly. I just can't see Stephen as the murderer. And why would George Morris be meeting a sixteen-year-old boy in the woods in the middle of the night?"

Exercise 10: Ergänzen Sie den Text mit den richtigen Präpositionen!
(at from in of in out)

Before the DI could answer, the two men became aware of an odd snuffling sound and a **rustling** 1. ________________ the undergrowth. They both fell silent and stood very still. To their amazement some leaves were pushed aside and a **badger** appeared 2. ____________ under a bush. Its black and white face stood 3. ________________ in the half-light 4. ________________ the early morning. For a long moment the badger and the policemen looked 5. ________________ each other 6. ________________ surprise.

Then the quiet of the woods was disturbed by the loud ringing of Sergeant Fox's mobile phone. He **frantically** searched through his pockets. He was hoping to turn it off before it scared off the badger, but he was too late, and they saw the badger's grey **fur** disappearing quickly back into the undergrowth.

rustling	Rascheln
badger	Dachs
frantically	verzweifelt
fur	Fell

Danny Fox put the phone to his ear in disappointment. He listened carefully before turning to his boss with growing excitement.
"Guess who is a member of George Morris' gun club!"

4 A Twist

"This makes the decision for us, Danny," said DI Billington. "We need to find Stephen. The boy might be frightened, but he could also be a murderer. Let's go."

Stephen answered the cottage door to Sergeant Fox's knock. His face lost all colour when he realized who it was. He looked back into the cottage as if he was thinking of running again. Sergeant Fox immediately grabbed hold of his arm.

"Don't even think about it. You won't be getting away this time."

"Put the handcuffs on him, Danny," said the Detective Inspector.

The boy was literally shaking with fear. As the cold metal fastened around his wrists, Stephen panicked.

"Mum! Mum! Don't let them take me."

handcuffs *pl*	Handschellen
literally	buchstäblich
tea towel	Geschirrtuch
half-shaved	halb rasiert
shaving foam	Rasierschaum

June Evans came running, a damp tea towel still in her hands. She stared in horror at the policemen with their hands on her child.

"What's going on? What are you doing to my son?"

Arthur Evans appeared at the top of the stairs. His face was half-shaved and he still had shaving foam on his left ear.

"You again!" he shouted. "Why are you back?"

Detective Inspector Billington nodded his head in a greeting.

"Mr Evans, we know you are a member of George Morris' gun club and keep a gun at home. Stephen was seen running away from the scene of the murder. He has access to a gun. He has some very serious questions to answer."

Arthur snorted as he came down the stairs to join them.

threatening	bedrohlich
indignant	empört
fool	Narr, Trottel
cabinet	Schrank
reluctantly	widerwillig

"The boy is stupid but he's not violent. He wouldn't have the courage. Don't make me laugh."
Arthur came to stand next to his wife and tried to look **threatening**.
"We know you own a gun, Mr Evans. We would like to see it," said DI Billington calmly. "Does Stephen have access to your gun? Could he have taken it without your knowledge?"
Arthur looked **indignant**.
"The little **fool** has never touched my gun. He wouldn't dare! I know the rules. My gun is properly locked away and the only key is always in my pocket. There is no way he can get to it. I'm the only one who uses it."

Exercise 11: Finden Sie das Gegenteil der Begriffe!

1. peaceful ______________________
2. clever ______________________
3. sunset ______________________
4. calm ______________________
5. fear ______________________
6. patience ______________________

"We still need to see it, Mr Evans."
Arthur Evans led the way to the back of the cottage and to a tall wooden **cabinet** in the corner of the lounge. He **reluctantly** handed

Sergeant Fox the key. Danny unlocked the door and carefully lifted the gun out of its cabinet.
"It's a shotgun, sir, and it looks like there is gunpowder residue on the gun barrel. This could mean it has recently been fired."
"Hmm, this changes things," said DI Billington. "Where were you, Mr Evans around 3 a.m. on the night George Morris was murdered?"
"I was in bed. Where do you think I would be at that time?"
"Is there anyone that can confirm this?"
Arthur nodded confidently at his wife.
"June can tell you. I never left the bedroom all night."
Detective Inspector Billington turned to the small anxious woman standing next to her son.
"Is this true, Mrs Evans?"
She hesitated and looked at her red-faced bully of a husband. Then slowly she shook her head.
"He was out," she whispered. "He took his shotgun. He told me he was shooting rabbits, but I don't know where he went."
Arthur let out a tremendous shout and leapt towards his wife.
"Why you...."
DI Billington stepped between them. June hid behind him.
"I suggest you calm down, sir."
"Calm down! Calm down?"
Arthur's voice was loud and indignant.
"I can't believe that you think I killed the man. George Morris was a liar and a cheat. He deserved everything he got. He never paid me

residue	Rest
barrel	Gewehrlauf
to confirm	bestätigen
confident	selbstsicher
anxious	ängstlich
to hesitate	zögern
tremendous	enorm, gewaltig
liar	Lügner
cheat	Betrüger

for the building work I did for him last summer. He **threatened** to take me to court. I did everything he had asked for. It's not my fault the gun club committee didn't like it. I had **kept my side of the bargain**. Is it too much to expect to get paid for the work I have done?"

to threaten	bedrohen
to keep one's side of the bargain	seinen Teil der Abmachung einhalten
by accident	aus Versehen
to lose one's temper	die Beherrschung verlieren

"Did you ever approach George and ask to be paid?"

Exercise 12: Lesen Sie weiter und setzen Sie die korrekte Verbform ein!

"Too right I did. He (1. stop) ____________ answering my phone calls so I (2. go) ____________ to see him at his house. His wife wouldn't let me in, but I (3. shout) ____________ and shouted until he (4. come) ____________ to the door. I (5. demand) ____________ my money and he threatened to set his dogs on me. His dogs! I should have called the police."

DI Billington gave the man a long, intense look.

"It seems you had a good reason to be angry with him. So what happened on the night George died? Did you meet **by accident** when you were out hunting rabbits? Did you have an argument and you **lost your temper**?"

fierce	wild, heftig
solemnly	ernst
hint	Hauch
support	Unterstützung
evidence	Beweis
sobbing	schluchzend

Arthur began to see where the conversation was heading. He tried to change his voice from a shout and to control his temper. "Now wait a minute. I didn't like the man and he owed me a lot of money, but I didn't kill him."

"You went to his house, Mr Evans. You were aggressive and you obviously have a fierce temper. Did you lose control and kill him when he wouldn't give you what you wanted?"

Arthur's face went purple.

"Now listen here, you idiot," he shouted. "I did not kill that cheat. How dare you come to my home and accuse me of murder! Get out of my house before I throw you out!"

"No, sir. We will be leaving, but I think you will be coming with us." Detective Inspector Billington stared solemnly at the man in front of him. Arthur Evans suddenly didn't look like such an aggressive bully. For once there was a hint of fear in his eyes. He looked to his wife for support, but she was staring at her feet and weeping quietly. She wouldn't raise her head.

"June?"

Arthur was unusually quiet as the Detective Inspector slipped the handcuffs around his wrists.

"Arthur Evans, I am arresting you for the murder of George Morris. You do not have to say anything, but anything you do say can be used as evidence against you."

Sergeant Fox released Stephen. The young man stood with his arm around his sobbing mother's shoulders as the policemen led his stepfather outside to the waiting police car.

Exercise 13: Beantworten Sie die Fragen zum Text!

1. Who did the policemen arrest first?

   ___

2. Where did Arthur tell his wife he was going on the night of the murder?

   ___

3. Why didn't Arthur like George?

   ___

4. Why was Arthur angry with his wife?

   ___

5 Guilty

DI Billington and Sergeant Fox were working on their paperwork back at the police station when Danny let out a sigh of disappointment.
"I have the lab report on Arthur Evans' shotgun here, sir. It says the gun has been recently fired, but it is not our murder weapon. It seems he was telling the truth about hunting rabbits."
"It looks that way, Danny," agreed the DI, "We don't have any more evidence against him. We will have to release him."
"So where does this leave us? We're right back at the beginning."
"Not necessarily. I think Stephen may still have some answers for us. Maybe we've just been asking the wrong questions."
Danny looked at his boss in confusion.
"What do you mean?"

paperwork	Papierkram
confusion	Verwirrung
to interrupt	unterbrechen
interview room	Verhörraum

"The boy has been in the woods and he is hiding something. We just need to work out what and why he won't tell us."
They were interrupted by a call from the station's receptionist. "Stephen McDougal and his mother are here and asking to speak to you."
Stephen and his mother were waiting at the reception desk. Away from her husband, Mrs Evans seemed to have grown more confident.
"Officers, Stephen has something to tell you."
The boy looked terrified.
"Okay," said DI Billington. "We need to do this formally. Follow me, please."
With Danny close behind him, the policeman led Stephen and his mother through the station and into an interview room. Once they

tape recorder	Kassettenrekorder
to shrink	*hier:* kleiner werden
to fiddle	*hier:* herumspielen

were sitting down, Sergeant Fox turned on the **tape recorder**.
"This is an interview with Stephen McDougal. The police officers present are Detective Inspector Charles Billington and Sergeant Daniel Fox. Stephen's mother June Evans is also here."
"Now," said the DI, "what is it you have come to say?"
Stephen's pale face went even whiter. He **shrank** into his seat. June took his hand and gave it an encouraging squeeze.
"It's alright, sweetheart. Nothing is going to happen to you. Now you must tell the officers what happened."
Stephen cleared his throat and began to speak in a quiet, trembling voice. He **fiddled** nervously with his fingers as he spoke.
"I was in the woods the night George Morris was killed."

Exercise 14: Ergänzen Sie die fehlenden Formen!

1. pale	____________	palest
2. ____________	closer	____________
3. ____________	____________	gentlest
4. bad	____________	____________
5. ____________	quieter	____________
6. ____________	more formal	____________
7. confident	____________	____________

to sneak out	sich heraus-schleichen
earth bank	Erdhügel
badger's sett	Dachsbau
miserably	unglücklich

The policemen exchanged a glance. Maybe this was the break they had been looking for. Stephen noticed the look.

"But I wasn't doing anything wrong!" he said earnestly. "Well, I know I wasn't supposed to be there. George had already warned me to stay away, but I wasn't hurting anyone."

"Let's not worry about that now," said Detective Inspector Billington in a sympathetic voice. "What were you doing in the woods, Stephen?"

The boy gave his mum a guilty look.

"I've been sneaking out at night," he admitted. "My mum and Arthur didn't know. A few weeks ago, I was out for a walk one day and I found a big hole dug into an earth bank. I thought something might live there, so I went back that night. It was a badger's sett and I watched them as they came out to hunt. I've been going back several nights a week since then."

"And that is why you were there the night George Morris was killed?"

"Yes. I know he told me to keep out of the woods. But I thought if I went at night then it would be okay. No one would ever know."

"Is this why you wouldn't speak to us before? You thought you would be in trouble?"

Again Stephen nodded miserably.

"Yes, and I was scared."

"Why scared? Did you see something the night George died? Did you see who murdered him?"

Stephen looked as if he wanted to run away or to disappear.

comfortingly	tröstend
ϟ **to pull oneself together**	sich zusammenreißen

"Go on, love," smiled June **comfortingly**. "You need to tell them what you know."

Exercise 15: Unterstreichen Sie alle Adverbien!

1. "Go on, Stephen," his mother prompted gently. "Tell the officers what you told me."
2. He fiddled nervously with his fingers as he spoke.
3. "But I wasn't doing anything wrong!" he said earnestly.
4. Again Stephen nodded miserably.
5. "Go on, love," smiled June comfortingly. "You need to tell them what you know."

The boy **pulled himself together** and continued.

"I was hiding in the bushes on the edge of the clearing. I didn't hear the men until it was too late for me to get away[i]. I couldn't move without them hearing or seeing me."

"What happened next?" asked Sergeant Fox.

"Their voices were quiet, but I could hear them coming closer. It was so dark I couldn't see them at first. Then they stepped out into the clearing and the moon shone on them."

"How many men were there and what did they look like?"

"There were two men to start with. They were wearing dark clothing and their hats were pulled down low. I couldn't see their faces. They just stood there like they were waiting for something."

Weitere Wendungen mit dem Verb **get** sind:

to get back	zurückkommen
to get around	herumkommen

content	Inhalt
wad	Bündel
to betray	betrügen
to refuse	sich weigern

The policemen nodded for him to keep talking.
"Then a third man appeared. He was carrying a big heavy bag. The first two men went to meet him. I couldn't hear what they were saying. The third man opened the bag to show them the contents. I couldn't see at first but then the moon shone on it and I could see as he took out a large, antique-looking gun."
"The stolen guns!" breathed Sergeant Fox.
"The men were exchanging a big wad of money when George Morris arrived. He must have seen the men's cars on the edge of the woods. He had come to see who was on his land. He was so angry when he recognized the man selling the guns. There was a big argument. George was furious. He kept shouting 'How could you betray me like this, after all this time?' He wanted them to give him the guns but they wouldn't. I suppose George was used to people doing as he told them. When they refused he tried to take the guns. There was a fight. The third man still had the gun in his hand. As George grabbed him the gun went off."
Stephen shut his eyes at the horrible memory.

Exercise 16: Ordnen Sie den Wörtern die passende Definition zu!

1. ☐ antique — a) to say no
2. ☐ badger — b) very angry
3. ☐ refuse — c) a valuable, old object
4. ☐ furious — d) an animal with a black and white face

"George fell to the floor. There was so much blood," he whispered. "The three men ran away into the woods."

"You're doing well, son," smiled DI Billington. "What happened next?"

Exercise 17: Lesen Sie weiter und unterstreichen Sie die richtige Variante!

"I waited until I was sure they had gone. Then I 1. (went / had gone) to see George. I 2. (doesn't / didn't) know what to do. I knew he was dead but I couldn't just 3. (let / leave) him there. I used my mobile phone to call for help. I waited 4. (at / in) the bushes until the police officers found him. Then I ran home."

"Why didn't you wait and talk to the police, Stephen?"

"I was scared. I wasn't supposed to be 5. (here / there) and I was worried they 6. (could / would) think I had done it."

"7. (Have / Did) you recognize any of the men, Stephen?" DI Billington asked. The boy nodded weakly.

"Yes, just one, the man 8. (who / which) shot George."

Thomas Cruickshank pulled his cap tightly down on the top of his head and stepped out into the gardens. He turned and locked the door of the shed at the back of the gun club. His shotgun was held loosely over his arm. As he moved out of the shadows of the doorway, his dog growled. Then he heard it.

"Drop your weapon, Mr Cruickshank, and put your hands on your head. We have you **surrounded**!"

to surround	umzingeln

Dressed to Die

Anne Ellsworth

1 A Horrible Discovery

The sun was setting over London in red and orange flames that made the rows of old buildings blush and glow. It had been another hot day in one of the longest heat waves the city had seen in the last decade. Now the streets were busy with after-work traffic; the drivers were trying to make it home to their cool, shady lawns as quickly as possible. The alleys were filled with pedestrians who were looking forward to a pleasant supper in one of London's many restaurants, coffee shops or fast-food places. Others were walking their dogs along the River Thames, now that the temperature had cooled down a little.

row	Reihe
to blush	erröten
glow	glühen
lawn	Rasen
recently	kürzlich, neulich
to glance	blicken, sich umsehen; (kurz) überfliegen

Jennifer Clearwater walked along the riverbank, dreaming about her trip to Bermuda. Was there anything she had forgotten to put on her list of things to put in the suitcase? Jeans, T-shirts, shorts, sandals, Jeffrey's bathing trunks, her own bathing suit... oh yes, and that pretty little bikini she had recently bought at "Gray's". It had pink and white stripes. "You look like a candy cane – sweet enough to eat," Jeffrey had remarked dryly when she had shown off her new two-piece bathing suit to him.

She could hardly wait to get on that airplane with her husband, whom she still adored even after seven years of happy marriage.

First she glanced at her watch, then she looked for Polly, their poodle, who had disappeared in the bushes by the water five minutes ago. "Pol-ly," she called. "Polly, come on, we've got to go now!"

faint	leise
high-pitched	schrill
twig	Zweig, Ast
to growl	knurren
pole	Mast, Pfahl
lead	Leine; Spur

No sight nor sound of Polly.

"Polly!" Jennifer called again. "Polly, come back, will you? Where are you, POLLY?!"

Suddenly she heard a faint bark behind her. It seemed to come from the river's edge. She stopped and turned round, walked back a few steps and listened. Yes, that definitely was Polly's high-pitched bark. "Yap! Yap! Yap!" She sounded excited and upset.

Jennifer pushed the twigs aside and ducked right through the hedges along the river, until she saw the water shimmering in the last sun rays of the day. "Polly!" she cried. The poodle responded with a series of excited barks from somewhere round the next bend.

The young woman walked hastily round the bend and saw her dog growl at something that looked like a long white branch floating in the water. No, it had to be something like a thick white pole because blue fabric, maybe a flag or tent or something else, was attached to it. This was what Polly was growling at – or rather pulling at.

"Polly! Come here! Let go of it, will you? We've got to go!"

The dog let go of the blue fabric but did not move from her spot. Instead she started on another series of barks.

"Polly! Leave that thing alone, will you? Come on, be a good doggy! We've got to go home to Daddy!"

Jennifer moved closer to put Polly on the lead and saw something that looked like a mop of wet black hair.

Then she froze. Oh my God, she thought. OH NO. It can't be! It couldn't... could it?

tangled	verwickelt, verflochten
to notify	benachrichtigen
to assign	zuweisen
investigation	Ermittlung
to drift	treiben
randomly	wahllos, zufällig, willkürlich
to mock	sich lustig machen
failure	Versagen

It was. It was another one of the Thames Murderer's victims. It was the body of a dead woman whose hair had got tangled in a bush. She was wearing a dress as blue as the sky.

Oh my God, Jennifer thought.

"Help!" she screamed. "Help! Murder! HELP!"

Then she grabbed Polly and ran back to civilisation to notify the police.

Shortly after six-thirty p.m. Inspector Hudson put down the receiver with a sigh. He had been expecting that phone call – in fact, he had been wondering for the past month or so when they would give up and assign him to the Thames Murder Case. Now he had both of them. And he didn't like it. No, sir, he didn't like it one bit. Because he had secretly been following up on Scotland Yard's investigations and felt that the murders of two beautiful young women, found drifting in the river, were tricky cases. Nothing linked the victims to each other, as far as he knew. The murderer seemed to pick them randomly in lonely parks after dark. They seemed to have nothing in common, except that the second woman had been found exactly four weeks after the first one. About a week after the first murder, a note had been sent to Scotland Yard, mocking their failure to find the murderer and signed "Jack the Skipper". Along with the letter, he had also sent the belt that belonged to the victim's dress. When the body was examined, it was found that the first victim had been strangled with that very belt.

eagerly	eifrig
to leaf through	durchblättern
capital	*hier:* Groß-
to shrug	mit den Schultern zucken
to fumble	fummeln
shiver	Schaudern, Zittern
spine	Rückgrat
evil	böse, teuflisch
murder weapon	Mordwaffe

What a horrible case, James Hudson thought.

There was a knock on his door.

"Come in," he called.

His secretary entered with a thick folder. "The Thames Murder Case, sir – they just brought it over."

"Thanks, I've been waiting for that."

Eagerly he took the heavy folder from her and leafed through it until he found the note the Yard had received one week after the first murder. It was handwritten in capital letters.

"Will that be all, sir?" she asked. "Because if you don't need me anymore, I would like to finish for the day. It's almost seven o'clock."

"What? Oh – yes, thank you," he answered without paying attention. His thoughts were on the note. The secretary shrugged and left, shutting the door behind her.

"Still fumbling in the dark, aren't you?" the note read. "You shouldn't be – it was bright enough when I strangled the poor lamb with this pretty beige belt, haha!"

Despite his many years of experience a cold shiver ran down his spine. He sensed he was about to deal with a very smart and evil mind and wondered if "Jack the Skipper" would again send the murder weapon together with another note.

On his way home Hudson could not stop thinking about the mocking note. His many years of dealing with all kinds of criminals told him that there was a hidden meaning between the lines. The note was too short for someone who wasted words. Why did the sender point out that it had been "bright" when he had strangled the woman? And what did he want to say with the name "Skipper"? Was the man they were looking for a sailor?

Exercise 1: Ordnen Sie die Wörter zu einem sinnvollen Satz!

1. heard Jennifer bark faint a suddenly her behind

   ____

2. like wet something looked hair a black mop of the

   ____

3. overlooked street he an woman almost crossing the old

   ____

4. today's murder would the reported newspaper be case in

   ____

5. old village a her parents in lived

   ____

6. he had the dresses looking been for were the connection

   ____

The inspector was so caught up in his thoughts that he almost overlooked an old woman crossing the street. He **frantically slammed on the brakes** and smiled an apology to the little old lady who was **furiously** shaking her umbrella at him.

"**Get a grip on yourself**, old man!" he told himself while wiping the sweat off his forehead.

frantically	hektisch, hastig, verängstigt
ϟ to slam on the brakes	eine Vollbremsung machen, ϟ auf die Bremse steigen

"Don't get too caught up in the case. You have to keep cool to find the bastard!"

furiously	energisch; wild
to get a grip on oneself	sich zusammenreißen, sich in den Griff bekommen
to scrape	kratzen
tray	*hier:* flache Schale, Auflaufform
to mumble	murmeln, nuscheln
to toss and turn	*hier:* sich (im Bett) hin und her wälzen
to be supposed to do sth.	etw. tun sollen
wreck	Wrack

When James Hudson finally got home at nine o'clock, he found Miss Paddington – his loyal housekeeper, cook, budget manager and drill sergeant – in the kitchen. She was busy scraping something black and burned out of a baking tray. The whole house smelled as if it had been set on fire.
"Oh my," she said nervously when she saw the inspector. "I'm afraid I burned our supper –"
"What is it?" he wanted to know. "Or rather – what WAS it?"
"Your favourite meal – my homemade pork pie," she mumbled without looking at him, scraping away furiously. "I'm so sorry but today just isn't my day! I didn't get any sleep last night. I tossed and turned and stayed awake all night – and today I'm completely useless!"
"You're never useless," Hudson replied politely, even though his stomach was growling hungrily, and right now he would have given anything for one of Miss Paddington's delicious pork pies.
"You're too kind, Inspector. But it's always the same when there is a full moon. I tried a cup of warm milk, and it didn't work. Then I even tried this special meditation that is supposed to make you tired no matter what. Oh yes, it made me tired alright! But I still couldn't fall asleep. Now I'm just a tired wreck."

"What did you just say?" the inspector asked absent-mindedly.
"I said I'm a tired wreck."
"No, I mean before that – did you say something about a 'full moon'?"

absent-mindedly	geistesabwesend, zerstreut
to dawn	dämmern
⚡ brains *pl*	*hier:* Grips, Verstand
to scramble	aufschlagen, verquirlen
to affect	beeinträchtigen

"Oh yes, the full moon! We had a full moon last night. Didn't you notice?"
Indeed Hudson, whose body did not care whether the moon was full or not, hadn't noticed. But now he remembered something.
"So last night was rather bright, wasn't it?" he inquired.
Miss Paddington looked at him as if she thought that his question was not too bright. "Yes, of course, Inspector. There were no clouds in the sky."
Hudson forgot his hungry stomach when something dawned on him.
"Why – of course!" he exclaimed. "Last night we had a full moon! That's what he meant with 'bright'! Miss Paddington, you're simply brilliant!"
The housekeeper was not too sure whether her beloved boss was still in his right mind or not. Could it be that the hot sun had scrambled his brains? Or perhaps the full moon had gotten to him? Maybe it affected people differently, so that some could not sleep (like her), while others could not think straight (like him)?
Hudson took one look at her and explained hastily: "Today they assigned the Thames Murder Cases to me. That's why I came home so late tonight. And as it turned out, the murderer seems to always

strike during a full moon, because a second victim was found early this evening."

"Oh my God, how horrible!"

Miss Paddington was so shocked she dropped the cooking pot she had been scrubbing. This was news to her. The media had not been told yet, because Scotland Yard had to notify the victim's family before the sad news could be made public.

to strike	(zu)schlagen
to strike gold	auf Gold stoßen; etw. Wichtiges herausfinden
to scrub	schrubben
to flatter	schmeicheln
to frown	die Stirn runzeln
to starve	(ver)hungern
shed new light on	ein neues Licht werfen auf
shift	Schicht

"Yes, and I wouldn't even have noticed if it hadn't been for your remark about the full moon! Perhaps I should retire and let YOU handle the case!"

That was a very flattering compliment, and for a second Miss Paddington smiled happily. Then she remembered her blackened pork pie and frowned.

"But, sir – I can't even serve you a proper supper tonight! And there is not enough food in the house to prepare something else. You must be starving by now!"

He really was starving, but he didn't want to make her feel any worse than she already felt. "Tell you what," he said. "Let's go out for a meal. I'm paying for it. After all it was you who shed new light on the Thames Murder Cases, Dr Watson!"

Early next morning Inspector Hudson found the autopsy report on his desk. The medical examiner had thrown in a late night shift because the second murder case would be reported in today's newspapers and on the local TV stations. The public was already starting to get hysterical about the Thames Murder Cases, and Scotland Yard had to come up with quick results – or at least with some details for the London public.

Exercise 2: Welches Wort ist das „schwarze Schaf"? Unterstreichen Sie!

1. sunset flames blush decade glow
2. supper pot scrub pork pie meal
3. keys handbag purse passport belt
4. agree ask murmur whistle answer
5. lead connection trace victim clue

He opened the report and read that this victim had also been strangled with a belt, or a similar object, as the strangulation marks on her neck showed. Then he looked at the photos of the victim. Her name was Sue Baker, and she had been a pretty young woman. The police had been able to identify her so quickly since the officers had discovered her handbag under a bush nearby. Nothing seemed to have been taken from the bag; her passport, her key chain and even her purse with a few bills and quite a lot of coins were all still there. She had been a waitress at the "Old Lion's Pub" and had taken home the tips received that evening. Since she had lived by herself, no one but her cat had yet noticed her **absence**. When the police officers notified her old parents, who lived in a village close to London, late last night, it was such a shock to her mother that she just

absence	Abwesenheit

to vow	schwören
responsible	verantwortlich
evidence	Beweis(stück)
sealed	versiegelt

kept asking over and over, "What about Lizzy? What about poor Lizzy?" Her husband explained that Lizzy was the name of Sue's cat. The officers had to drive over to Sue's flat and fetch a very scared and hungry cat. After they had dropped the animal off at the parents' home, Sue's mother seemed to calm down a bit.

These are the tragedies behind the breaking news of a spectacular crime, Hudson thought. The personal tragedies usually don't make the news. However, they do make me care about my cases.

He silently vowed to himself that he would find the person who was responsible for the tragedy of Sue Baker's mother – and Lizzy, the cat.

"Just a moment." The young officer disappeared between the long shelves on which the evidence was kept in sealed plastic bags. A minute later he returned with three labelled packages.

"Here you go, sir." He handed the plastic bags over to Inspector Hudson. Inside were the two dresses the victims had been wearing last and the belt "Jack the Skipper" had sent with his note. The beige dress of the first victim clearly matched the belt the young woman had been strangled with. The inspector looked at the label inside the dress. It was a French designer he had never heard of. Clearly the dress had been expensive.

He took a photograph of the label.

Curiously he turned to the second dress. This one was of a deep blue.

"Did it come with a belt?" he asked the young officer.

The officer shook his head. "No, sir, no belt came with that piece of evidence."

to make ends meet	über die Runden kommen
coincidence	Zufall

Hudson glanced at the label. It was the same French designer. He whistled through his teeth.

"The same type of dress as the first one? That's strange," James Hudson murmured in surprise. "And a waitress in expensive French designer clothes? That's even stranger..."

"Yes, sir, isn't it?" the young officer agreed. "You'd think they don't earn enough money to **make ends meet** – and then go out and buy a French dress like that? Oh well, you never know with women –"

But Hudson was no longer listening. He didn't know very much about women, but he DID know that the similarity of those two dresses was no **coincidence**. They were a lead. An important new lead in the Thames Murder Cases. They tied the two cases together. They were the connection he had been looking for.

Exercise 3: Beantworten Sie die Fragen zum Text!

1. What was Jennifer Clearwater looking forward to?

   ____

2. What had "Jack the Skipper" sent after the first murder?

   ____

3. Why did Miss Paddington burn her pork pie?

   ____

4. How were the two women killed?

   ____

5. Who was the only one who noticed Sue Baker's absence?

   ____

2 Two Dresses in a Desert

The next person on Hudson's list was Elvira Elliot, his favourite insurance investigator. She also happened to be his favourite person; but that was something he would never admit to himself or anyone else.

"You're lucky," Elvira said as soon as he had identified himself on the phone. "I was just leaving my office."

"Then I am lucky indeed," James Hudson said, feeling stupid. Why did she always make him feel like a clumsy schoolboy? Perhaps Miss Paddington knew the answer to that question. But then again – better not ask her. She might think all the wrong things.

insurance investigator	Versicherungs-vermittler(in)
clumsy	ungeschickt
sultry voice	tiefe Stimme, erotische Stimme
to wipe	(ab)wischen, (ab)reiben

"Glad you see it that way, too," Elvira said in her sultry voice. She sounded amused.

Hudson noticed how hot it was in his office and wiped the sweat off his forehead. "Well, I just have a short question," he said a touch too rudely.

"What is it, Inspector?" Whenever she called him by his title and not by his first name, it put him in a bad mood. He didn't know why and he didn't care to know why, either.

"Does the name 'Petite Fleur du Jardin' ring a bell?" he asked.

"'Petite fleur du jardin'? Did you just call me 'little flower of the garden', Inspector? How sweet of you! I didn't know you could be romantic," Elvira said in that sultry voice of hers. He just KNEW that she was being sarcastic.

peach	Pfirsich; pfirsichfarben
gruffly	mürrisch, grob
to sob	schluchzen
to usher into	hineinführen
overstuffed	gut gepolstert
array	*hier:* Strauß; Arrangement, Anordnung
grieving	trauernd

"It's a French designer label," he explained, and again he felt like a fool.

"Ah yes, now I remember," Elvira replied. "Yes, that's a very expensive French dressmaker. You only get those dresses at 'Gray's'. I think they sell the whole summer collection there. I simply MUST get myself one soon! Should I get one in peach or in navy blue – what do you think, James?"

"Don't ask me," he said. Elvira would look good in any colour of the rainbow, he thought.

At least this time she had not called him by his title...

"Thanks for your help," he said gruffly.

"Any time, sir," she replied and hung up.

When Mrs Baker opened the door to let the Scotland Yard inspector in, she began to cry. "Poor Lizzy," she sobbed, "she hasn't been eating anything! It's not very nice of Sue to leave her cat alone for so long, is it?"

"She's still not quite herself," Mr Baker explained to Hudson, while he ushered the inspector into the living room.

Hudson sat down on an overstuffed sofa. Its cover was a mixed array of pink roses, white lilies and green ferns. Little flowers in a garden... it reminded him of the first question he had to ask the grieving parents.

"I'm sorry to bother you," he said. "But I need to ask you if Sue recently bought a blue French designer dress."

Mr Baker shook his head, and his wife burst out in tears again. "A French dress? Aren't they expensive? I don't think so," the father said. "We raised our girl to be modest."

"She always bought cat food with the tips she got from the guests over at the pub," his wife sobbed. "She took such good care of Lizzy. That's why I can't understand why she hasn't come back for her cat yet..."

"Did Sue have a boyfriend? Was she seeing anyone?" the inspector continued.

"No," her father replied. "As far as we know, she only had a few girlfriends. Sometimes they would go out for a meal or a film. Sue didn't have any time for a man – she had to work most evenings anyway."

"Could she have met a man at the 'Old Lion's Pub'?" Hudson wanted to know. "Someone who might have bought her a blue French designer dress?"

Again Mr Baker shook his head. "I think she would have told us," he said sadly. "But she did not mention any special man in her life."

"She was such a pretty girl," his wife sobbed. "And she loved pretty clothes. But she didn't have the money for expensive dresses. She was saving most of her money for veterinary school. You see, she wanted to become a veterinarian."

Sue's father nodded proudly. "Yes, my little girl would have made a fine veterinarian." His voice broke.

Sue's mother shook her head and mumbled, "But now I'm no longer sure about that. Why did she leave her poor cat alone? That's not very nice of her, is it?"

The inspector rose. He did not want to bother the grieving par-

veterinary	tierärztlich

ents any more for the time being. "Thank you so much," he said. "I'll do everything to find the person who did this to your daughter. I promise."

The first victim's name was Melanie Jordan. She had been a 28-year-old secretary. On the night she was murdered she had gone out with an old schoolfriend. They had spent a pleasant but unspectacular evening in the city, and shortly after twelve she had said goodbye to her friend. The next morning a dock worker had found her on the banks of the River Thames – strangled and wearing that beige dress.

pleasant	angenehm
dock worker	Hafenarbeiter
witness	Zeuge, Zeugin

Of course Hudson's colleagues had already interviewed her family, friends and co-workers. But there was a new question they had not asked yet simply because it had not come up before.

He made a few phone calls. "Did Melanie recently buy a beige French designer dress?" he asked one witness after another.

"Not that I know of," her best friend said.

"She couldn't afford expensive clothes," her mother said.

"She didn't wear a beige dress that night," her old schoolfriend said. "Let me see – oh yes, she was dressed in jeans and a red cotton top. She had taken along a jacket, but she didn't put it on because the evening was so mild."

Looks like the man who killed the two women is also the man who bought those two dresses, Hudson thought. The same man who sent us the belt and calls himself "Jack the Skipper".

Again he wondered if there would be another note soon. And another murder after that.

Exercise 4: Übersetzen Sie folgende Aussagen!

1. He stepped into another world.

   ____

2. The woman saw him look at her purchase.

   ____

3. Her features were a bit hard.

   ____

4. I showed him the dress in all colours.

   ____

5. The customer seemed to be particularly interested in the blue dress.

   ____

On the outside "Gray's" was an unspectacular building in one of the narrow side streets found in West End. It had a fresh white **coat of paint.** The window frames and the beautiful old wooden door were painted blue. Only a small **brass** sign over the heavy door which read "Gray's Boutique" told the inspector that he was entering the right shop.

He stepped into another world. The high walls and the ceiling were as blue as the sky. The far wall was decorated with some abstract paintings. The floor was covered with white sand. There were three tall potted palm-trees in different corners. Dresses, skirts, blouses, trousers and jackets were arranged on hangers that hung from thick white **ropes** along the other three walls. A sandy-

coat of paint	Farbanstrich
brass	Messing
rope	Seil

coloured wooden booth in the form of a pyramid was in the centre of the large sales room. Its shelves were filled with jumpers, T-shirts and accessories. An old brass **cash register** was sitting on a small wooden table in front of the pyramid.

Exotic music was coming from somewhere. Hudson looked round but he could not see any **speakers**. The music seemed to be coming from behind the potted palms.

A woman left the row of colourful blouses she had been admiring. "Don't you just love their desert theme?" she asked while passing him to look at the next row of colourful blouses.

"What? Oh yes, certainly," he said. "It's rather – creative!"

The only thing that's missing is a camel, he thought to himself.

A young shop assistant dressed in white shorts, a white top and white sandals came up to him. "May I help you, sir?" she asked. "Is there anything particular you're looking for?"

"No – I mean, yes – I'm looking for the manager." He showed her his **badge**. "Inspector James Hudson from Scotland Yard."

cash register	Kasse
speaker	*hier:* Lautsprecher
badge	Polizeiabzeichen
flustered	eingeschüchtert; verwirrt

"Scotland Yard?" the young assistant asked shocked. "Why – what's wrong?"

"Would you please just get the shop manager?" Hudson said patiently.

"Oh yes, of course, sir." The **flustered** girl ran off.

The woman who had been inspecting her third row of blouses turned round. Still holding up a very pink blouse, she glanced at the inspector. "The Yard here at 'Gray's'? What are you looking for – an illegally imported camel?"

"Not really." Hudson shook his head. "But if I were you, I would stay away from that pink!"
Without so much as another glance she marched off to a row of pastel ensembles.
Half a minute later the flustered shop assistant returned with the flustered shop manager. "Emily Gray," she introduced herself nervously. "I'm the owner of the shop. How may I help you?"

pastel	Pastellton
ensemble	*hier:* zusammen-passende Klei-dungsstücke, Kombination
in reference to	bezüglich, in Bezug auf
to brush back	*hier:* aus der Stirn streichen
unique	einzigartig
desert	Wüste
features *pl*	Gesichtszüge; Eigenschaften; Kennzeichen

"I need to ask you some questions in reference to an investigation," Hudson explained. "Is there a room where we could talk privately?"
"Oh, of course! Please come along this way." Ms Gray led the inspector into her office and offered him a seat. Then she sat down and brushed back her long black hair.
"So what brings you here?" she asked businesslike. "Surely not our unique desert theme?"
The inspector studied her for a second. She was a good-looking woman about forty, even though her features were a bit hard. But then it probably was hard work to keep a trendy boutique like this one successful year after year. Aloud he said, "No, of course not – although it certainly is impressive! But the reason for my stopping by are the two murder victims we found on the banks of the Thames. I'm sure you've heard about them?"
"Oh yes, I read in 'The Times' that they found another poor woman yesterday, didn't they? How horrible!" She shook her head in

purchase	kaufen
garment	Kleidungsstück
aghast	entgeistert, entsetzt
enclosed	beigelegt, beigefügt
culprit	Täter(in), Schuldige(r)

disbelief. "Who would do something like that?"

"That's what I'm here to find out. You see, the dresses the two women were wearing when they were found both have the label 'Petite Fleur du Jardin'. I understand you carry that label in your collection?"

"'Petite Fleur du Jardin'?" Emily Gray asked shocked. "Are you sure? Yes, we carry that label in this year's summer collection. But what does that have to do with –" she paused thoughtfully. "Oh my God, of course! Now I understand. 'Gray's' is the only place in all of London that sells 'Petite Fleur du Jardin' models! That's why it's been so successful here. But the fact that the victims purchased those dresses here doesn't tell you anything about their murderer yet, does it?"

Hudson shook his head. "No, that's exactly the point. They did not buy the dresses! These garments are completely unknown to the victims' families, friends or co-workers! It seems that the murderer has made them put on these dresses shortly before he killed them."

Ms Gray looked aghast. "My dresses? He made them put on my dresses? My beautiful 'Petite Fleur du Jardin' dresses? What a beast! How did he kill them? The papers didn't say anything about that."

Inspector Hudson was not going to say anything about that, either. The media had not been informed of the note by "Jack the Skipper" and the enclosed belt. This was information that only the police knew – and the culprit himself.

"That's not important now, Ms Gray," he said. "What's important is to know who bought those dresses at your shop. I need you to check your bookkeeping to make sure that no dresses were stolen. And I will also need two dresses of the exact colours the victims were wearing."

bookkeeping	Buchhaltung
personnel	Personal
sample	Muster(stück)
ruffled	gerüscht
slim	schmal, schlank

Ms Gray said uncertainly, "I'm not sure if my sales personnel will actually remember the customer who bought those dresses. But I certainly can help you out with the sample dresses. What colours are they?"
"One is beige, and the other one is a kind of a brilliant dark blue."
"Oh yes, I know which ones you are talking about. The unicoloured V-neck dresses with the ruffled skirt and the slim belt! Those sell really well – why, we must have sold at least ten of each. That's because they are very reasonably priced for one hundred percent of pure silk and such a flattering cut. Let me show you." She rose from her chair and walked to the door.

Exercise 5: Setzen Sie die richtige Zukunftsform **will, going** oder **is going to** ein!

1. It's getting cold, I ______________ close the window.
2. Hudson ______________ talk to Dr Walsch tomorrow.
3. By this time tomorrow the inspector ______________ know more.
4. There is no time left; he ______________ have to talk to her later.
5. Hudson is actually ______________ straight back to the police station.
6. On Friday at 11 o'clock we are ______________ to the funeral.
7. Oh no! I think Mrs Lyons ________________ hit the Inspector!

The inspector followed her back into the sales room, past the cash register. The woman who had been so interested in blouses was just paying for her newest treasure. Hudson noticed with a quick glance that she had not picked the pink blouse but one in a greyish green. She looked up and saw him look at her purchase.
"Very pretty," he nodded grinning. "It's definitely you!"
"Have you found the camel yet, Inspector?" she replied. "You may want to check out the dressing cabins!" Grabbing her shopping bag, she walked out the door.
All four shop assistants were completely dressed in white to match the desert theme, but they could not remember a man buying the dresses in question.
"One or two women were accompanied by their husband or boyfriend," Mandy said. "But I can't remember selling those dresses to any male customer."

✧ chap	✧ Kerl, Bursche

Jacqueline could not remember whom she had sold any of the dresses to, and Sandy could not even remember selling any dresses to anyone.
But Bernadine remembered something. "Oh yes, there was this chap who came in a few months ago at the beginning of the summer season. I remember that because back then we still had these dresses in all colours. We had not sold very many yet."
"Yes, and?" the inspector asked impatiently. "Did he buy one or more dresses? What did he say he wanted them for? What did he look like?"
Bernadine shook her head. "No, he didn't buy any dress. But he kept going back to the blue ones. It's called Summer Sea. I showed him the dress in all colours, but he seemed to be particularly inter-

to roll	rollen; (Augen) verdrehen

ested in the blue one. He even took it outside and held it into the daylight. But then he put it back and said his wife had better try it on first, since she was very particular about colours."

"Did he look at the beige one as well?"

"You mean this one? Sahara Sand?" The girl frowned while she was trying to remember. "No. Actually he was only interested in the blue one and the green one. That one is called Cool Mint – but he was more interested in the blue one."

"What did he look like? Was he tall or short? Blond or dark? How old would you say he was? Did he wear glasses? How was he dressed?" the inspector wanted to know.

"He was – I don't know, normal, I guess. I mean he wasn't particularly good-looking."

"She only notices the good-looking ones," Jacqueline remarked.

Hudson **rolled** his eyes. "Can you remember anything else about that man? Old or young? Anything?" he asked.

Bernadine was thinking hard. "He must have been about thirty or thirty-five at the most. Oh yes – he wore glasses with golden frames! And he was kind of dirty blond. He was neither tall nor short, kind of in between."

"Well, thank you, that's excellent," Hudson said. "Specially since that chap wasn't good-looking, I mean."

Jacqueline grinned at him, but Bernadine had not noticed his sarcasm. She was smiling happily.

3 A Dead Rose and Two Artists

At noon the next day Ms Gray called Hudson. She told him that she had personally checked her **records** of the last months.

"Nothing, Inspector," she reported. "The only thing that is unaccounted for is an old **dummy** we don't use any more anyway."

"A dummy?" he asked. "Who would steal a dummy?"

"I have no idea. It had been collecting **dust** in the **storage** room, and then one day it was gone. Perhaps it walked off by itself."

"When did it disappear?" Hudson asked more out of **habit** than interest.

"Oh, about the time I came down with the flu. Let me see – that must have been round Easter," the shop owner **stated**. "Now I compared all sales to our **inventory** of clothes. Nothing is missing, not one single **item** that might have been stolen. All clothes were properly paid for."

records *pl*	Unterlagen, Akten
dummy	*hier:* Schaufensterpuppe
dust	Staub
storage	Lager, Lagerung
habit	Gewohnheit
to state	feststellen; aussagen
inventory	Inventar
item	*hier:* Posten; Gegenstand

"What about cheques and credit cards? How long do you keep records of those?" Hudson asked.

"Forever," she said. "They're still all there. But do you really think the murderer would have paid for those dresses with a cheque or credit card?"

"No, I don't," he replied truthfully. "But we have to investigate every possible lead, you know."

"Yes, I understand that," the boutique owner said. "But this will be handled discreetly, won't it? I don't want the police to upset my

to assure	versichern, zusichern
handy	*hier:* griffbereit; handlich; praktisch
figures *pl*	Zahlen
shipyard	Schiffswerft
shortcut	Abkürzung

customers – it might ruin the good reputation of my shop!"
"Of course we will be discreet about it," the inspector **assured** her. "I will personally see to that. So could you keep all your records **handy,** so that one of my men can pick them up this afternoon? You will get everything back as soon as we are finished with it – the two dresses as well."
She promised to have everything ready to be picked up in the afternoon. Just before she was about to hang up, the inspector said: "Oh, just one more question – who has keys to your shop and the storage area?"
"Only myself. I am always the first person to get there and the last one to leave."
"Sounds just like my job," Hudson remarked. "Thank you so much. Goodbye."
"Goodbye, Inspector." She hung up.
Well, this is one job I won't handle myself, Hudson thought. Sorting through bookkeeping records and dealing with **figures** is just not my cup of tea! Let me see – who will be the lucky one to take care of "Gray's" bookkeeping?

The heatwave had finally cooled off and was replaced by rain. The water was pouring down from the sky as if God Himself was taking a long, refreshing shower.
Hudson drove out of the city centre and past the Updike **Shipyard** by the river. He took the **shortcut** through the industrial area and then some side roads that finally led to the wealthy part of town

where he lived. His house was small but exquisite and surrounded by a large lawn and a rose garden, which was his housekeeper's great passion.

It's raining cats and dogs!	Es regnet in Strömen.
sip	Schluck
cinnamon	Zimt
to spoil	*hier:* verwöhnen; verderben
blossom	Blüte
How fitting!	Wie passend!

"It's raining cats and dogs!" Miss Paddington said as a sort of welcome when Hudson opened the front door.

"Who are you telling this? I feel like shaking myself like a wet poodle." He had to sneeze.

Miss Paddington hurried off to the kitchen and returned with a steaming cup of hot chocolate. "Here you go. Just what the doctor ordered."

He gratefully drank a few sips. His housekeeper always seemed to know what he needed at that moment. "Thank you," he said. "That's delicious."

"It's made with real cocoa and a touch of cinnamon. My Aunt Libby taught me how to make it when I was a young girl."

"Well, God bless Aunt Libby's soul," the inspector said. "May she spoil all the angels in heaven with her hot chocolate!"

"Hope you don't catch a cold, Inspector. But to be honest – I'm glad we finally get some rain after all that sun."

"You're right. I was starting to feel as if I'm in Florida instead of in good old England!" Hudson said ironically.

"That's not what I mean. But the roses did not take very well to all that heat. And they are my first painting project. I'm working on a still life – a perfect single rose blossom in a glass vase. I'll call it 'Rose in Glass'."

"How fitting," the inspector remarked dryly.

"Yes, isn't it?" she said proudly. "But before I could finish, all the blossoms died on me because of the hot weather."
"Then why don't you just call the painting 'Dead Rose in Glass'? Or you could call it 'Rose Dying in Glass'."
Miss Paddington did not like it when the inspector made jokes like that. "That's not funny, Inspector. You've had too many death investigations," she said curtly. "And being all by yourself doesn't help either, you know. Have you seen that nice lady lately? What's her name – Elvira?"
Having made her point, the housekeeper took his empty cup and left him by himself to think about that nice lady, Elvira.
Perhaps I should get a cat, he thought. They are just as complicated as women. And they have just as long claws. But you don't have to impress them with compliments.

curtly	kurz angebunden
claw	Kralle, Klaue
impress	beeindrucken
to boost	stärken, fördern
to display	zeigen, darstellen
ϟ So what?	ϟ Na und?
to confirm	bestätigen

Inspector Hudson was no longer thinking about cats. He was thinking about the stranger one of the shop assistants had mentioned. How to find the male customer who had shown such interest in the blue dress? Well, the only way to do that was through the media. The shop owner would probably not be too thrilled about that. But then it might even boost her business if the dresses were displayed attractively inside the store.
Oh, so what, he thought. We will even mention that desert theme. That should make her happy.
The young investigator who had to sort through "Gray's" bookkeeping records confirmed what the boutique owner had already

told Hudson. Everything was totally correct. No dress could be missing from the inventory.

Exercise 6: Ordnen Sie die Wörter zu einem sinnvollen Satz!

1. by replaced the rain finally was wave heat

___

2. attractively the dresses inside were store displayed the

___

3. discuss didn't artwork the here come to inspector the

___

4. Gray himself poured a freshly of made lemonade glass

___

5. herself is living an lady old by she

___

6. the papers perhaps he not did read

___

"We're still checking into the **purchases** that were made on credit card or by cheque, sir. So far the customers have been able to show us what they bought at 'Gray's'. We're only waiting on three more customers who couldn't be reached yet. By the way," the young officer continued, "the woman who found the second victim – her name is Jennifer Clearwater – is among 'Gray's' customers. We are still waiting for the results there, because she and her husband are on

purchase	Kauf

holiday right now. But the **amount** she paid by credit card is less than the price they ask for one of those dresses. So it can't have been a dress she bought. The shop assistants think it was a bikini or something like that."

amount	Betrag
to flush	*hier:* erröten
subordinate	Untergebene(r)
lamely	lahm
therefore	daher, deshalb
favour	Gefallen
immediately	sofort

"So that's not a lead," the inspector said, shaking his head. "Actually, so far every lead has turned into a dead end. Well, get back to me as soon as you have talked to the remaining customers. And thank you. You're doing a good job."

The young officer **flushed** with surprise. "Why, thank you, sir!" he said and hurried off to do an even better job.

Why is it so much easier to compliment a **subordinate** on a job well done than it is to pay a compliment to a beautiful woman? The inspector wondered.

"You always call when I'm in a hurry," Elvira said. "How do you always know when I'm getting ready to leave?"

"I don't," Hudson replied **lamely**. "Sorry to bother you again so soon. But we're not getting anywhere in the Thames Murder Cases. All we know is that the murderer must have bought the dresses at Gray's – or somewhere far away in another big city. This 'Petite Fleur du Jardin' stuff is only sold in a few very exclusive shops, as we found out. **Therefore** I need your help."

He sighed. He liked to call Elvira, but he hated to have to ask any **favours** of her.

She seemed to have heard his sigh, because her voice softened **immediately**. "How can I help you out? I don't know any more about those dresses than you already do."

"But you socialize with the kind of people who buy clothes like that. People who can afford those prices, I mean. We're probably looking for someone with money – some clown who can go out and buy two very expensive dresses just for the thrill. And the kill, so to speak."

"Nice wordplay, James," Elvira said. "But a sad subject."

"That's how I feel, too. I have to find the bastard before he strikes again!"

"What makes you think he will strike again?"

The inspector could not tell her about the pattern he was beginning to see – the full moon and the same type of dress. "Let's just call it an instinct. I have a feeling he will kill again. And soon."

"Tell you what. I will see what I can find out. I will ask all my friends in high places a few discreet questions – without mentioning you, of course. By the way, how did you like the paintings?"

to socialize	verkehren, befreundet sein
to afford	leisten
subject	Thema; Subjekt
pattern	Muster
divorced	geschieden
twin	Zwilling
abstract	*hier:* abstraktes Gemälde

"What paintings?" He had no idea what she was talking about.

"The paintings in 'Gray's' boutique. O.U. Gray's paintings. Didn't you see them? Three of them are hanging on one of the walls. They bear his artist's initials O.U.G."

"O.U. Gray's paintings? Who is O.U. Gray? Ms Gray's husband?" he asked in confusion. "But she said she was divorced."

"O.U. Gray is her twin brother," Elvira explained patiently. "He is a very talented local artist, very 'in' at the moment. Does abstracts. He has developed his own soft, flowing style. So his pictures always

peachy	pfirsichfarben, -ähnlich
to stutter	stottern
to chuckle	glucksen, leise kichern
stiffly	steif, verkrampft

look as if they were taken under water. Some critics already call him a genius."

The inspector, who could not tell the difference between a rose in a glass from an abstract rose under water, was surprised. Ms Gray had not mentioned that she had a brother. So there was another man around who could have somehow taken those dresses!

"Elvira?"

"What, oh James?" she asked in her sultry voice that made him want to call her more often.

"You know what? You just gave me an important new lead! O.U. Gray! I had no idea about the man! Thank you – thank you so much!"

"You're quite welcome. But now I've got to run."

She wanted to hang up on him, but he stopped her just in time. "One more thing," he said.

"What is it?"

"Tha-that **peachy** dress you were thinking of buying? I saw it in the shop," he **stuttered**. "And you would look great in it."

"Are you sure now?" she sounded amused.

"No, I mean yes – I mean b-beautiful. I really wanted to say that you would look beautiful in that peach-coloured dress. Like a beautiful peach."

"You mean like a 'petite pêche du jardin'?" she **chuckled**.

"Well, I didn't mean it as a joke," he said **stiffly**.

"James, that was the sweetest compliment I ever heard. No one has ever called me a 'beautiful peach'! Now I will definitely have to buy

to ring off	auflegen (Telefon)
to savour	genießen
jug	Krug

it. It's all your fault if I spend half of my monthly income on that peachy dress! Have a nice day!"

They **rang off**.

He had done it. He had paid her the sweetest compliment she had ever heard. James Hudson leaned back in his office chair, doing nothing but **savour** the moment.

Exercise 7: Welche Wörter gehören zusammen?

1. garment	☐ upset
2. rose	☐ lemonade
3. jug	☐ dress
4. irritated	☐ belt
5. liquid	☐ expensive
6. accessories	☐ glass
7. afford	☐ blossom

O.U. Gray had the same black hair, blue eyes and features as his twin sister Emily, but his face was softer and he seemed younger than her. He was dressed casually in jeans and a black jersey shirt. Now he is a man that young Bernadine probably considers good-looking, James Hudson thought. But he doesn't look as if he could run a successful business the way his sister does.

"Come on in, Inspector." Gray led Hudson into his living room. "Do you care for a cup of Orange Pekoe or a glass of lemonade?" He pointed at a glass **jug**.

"No, thank you. I won't take up much of your time. I just have a few questions."
Gray poured himself a glass of freshly made lemonade. He took a sip of the pale yellow **liquid**. "So what brings the famous Scotland Yard Inspector Hudson here to my **modest** home?"
"I wouldn't exactly call it modest," Hudson replied, looking round the huge room with the high ceiling. The walls, the marble floor and the leather furniture were all white. A few white decorative vases were placed here and there. Even the photo books on the coffee table had white covers. The only **splash of colour** in the room was a great big rug in the centre of the room. All colours of the rainbow were woven into its beautiful pattern.

liquid	Flüssigkeit
modest	einfach, bescheiden
splash of colour	Farbfleck, Farbtupfer

Pointing at it, the inspector remarked, "That's a nice piece. It looks like an Indian pattern."
"It is," Gray nodded. "I bought it at an Indian reservation in Arizona. It is handmade, and the colours are all natural. No chemicals at all."
"Very beautiful," Hudson commented. "But I don't see any paintings on the walls. I heard you're an artist who has made quite a name of himself."
Gray put down his glass and smiled. "Who told you that? That's a bit of an exaggeration, I'd say. I'm just using my own watercolour technique, that's all. And I don't like to display my own art in my own living room. It's like bringing your work home if you know what I mean."
Either he really is too modest – or he thinks so highly of himself that he does not want anyone to know what he really thinks of his

easygoing	umgänglich; locker, gelassen
genuinely	*hier:* aufrichtig; echt
to suspect	verdächtigen
to eliminate	ausschließen; auslöschen

own art, Hudson thought. But the man seemed nice and **easy-going** enough.

"Well, I'm sure you didn't come here to discuss artwork, did you? So what brought you here, Inspector?"

"I'm investigating into the Thames Murder Cases," Hudson replied. "I need to ask you what you did three nights ago – Sunday night between eleven p.m. and three a.m. on Monday morning."

Gray looked **genuinely** shocked. "That sounds as if – as if you suspect ME of killing those poor women! But that's totally absurd! What did I do to be suspected of such a horrible act?"

"I didn't say we **suspect** you or anyone else, for that matter," the inspector said calmly. "I just have to **eliminate** all persons who could have anything to do with the two crimes. So what did you do during the time in question?"

Frowning, Gray stared at the white ceiling. "Let me see," he said thoughtfully. "When did you say it was – Sunday night? What did I do that night? Oh yes – it was really hot that day, and so I spent the whole day by the pool at my sister's house. After supper I went home. That was about ten o'clock. Then I worked a bit on a painting and watched a late film on television. An American film; it was called 'The Magic Touch'. After that I went to sleep. That was about 3:30 a.m."

"So you were by yourself? Or can anyone verify what you just told me?"

Gray shook his head. "No, I'm afraid not. I was by myself. But that's absurd, Inspector! I can tell you what happened in the film –"

"That won't do. You could have **taped** it on a video recorder and watched it later, you see? That's not an alibi."
Gray jumped up and walked over to the window. He was clearly **irritated** and upset. "I have nothing to do with those horrible murders!" he exclaimed. "Had I known that some woman would get killed Sunday night and that I would be suspected, I would have made sure to get myself a watertight alibi!" He stared out of the window and suddenly turned round. "But wait – my neighbour! She may have seen me paint in my studio! Ask her if she saw me through the curtains. And I always listen to pop music while I paint. Sunday night I put on some music. I kept the window open, because it was still so hot in the flat. I believe she also kept her window open, so she may have seen me paint and heard me sing along to the music."

to tape	*hier:* einen Film aufnehmen
irritated	irritiert, verärgert

The inspector got up. "Yes, I'll do that. She may be your alibi. Say, do you have any keys to your sister's boutique?"
"No, sir. Why should she give me a spare key? I have nothing to do with her business. Unfortunately I'm not good with money and figures. I never developed the left side of my brain, I guess." He smiled and shrugged. "My mother always wanted me to become a businessman. Now I paint abstract watercolours. Oh well, you can't please them all, can you?"
"No, you can't," the inspector said. "Well, thank you so much for your time, Mr Gray. We'll see what your neighbour has to say. What's her name?"
"Mrs Kennedy, I believe. I don't know her very well; we just say hello when we meet downstairs. She is an old lady living by herself."

barely	*hier:* kaum
flee the scene	(vom Tatort) flüchten
clue	Spur, Anhaltspunkt, Indiz
suspicious	verdächtig

The old lady did remember seeing Gray through the white cotton curtains of his window. "Yes, sir, he was sitting there painting all right when I was watering my balcony flowers before going to bed at half past eleven. In that heat you have to water them twice a day, you know? And the young gentleman over there was concentrating on his painting, singing. Mind you, he wasn't being loud, he has very good manners. You could barely hear him. He's really well-educated. And in addition, he is good-looking, too. I wonder why he hasn't married by now. Of course most young women have a job these days, but that isn't what they're really after, is it? I think they still want to get married, deep down in their hearts, I mean..."
Inspector Hudson hastily thanked her and fled the scene.

The final results of the check-up on "Gray's" customers who had paid by cheque or credit card did not offer any new clues, either. All the purchases of dresses, blouses, skirts and bikinis matched up. "I couldn't find anything that looks suspicious, sir," the young investigator reported to Hudson. "Only two women bought one of those blue dresses on credit card – and both still have their dress and the belt that comes with it, as they showed me. One woman bought a beige dress and paid with a cheque. But she still has the complete garment as well, and she just bought it two weeks ago."
"Then that was after the first murder," the inspector murmured and shook his head. "This is leading us nowhere. But thank you anyhow."

to be keen on	↯ scharf auf, wild auf

Thursday morning the "London Times" ran a short article on the male customer who had shown such interest in the blue "Petite Fleur du Jardin" dress a few months before. The article only said that he may be an important witness to the two crimes and should report to Scotland Yard immediately. The paper also printed two pictures. One displayed the blue dress on a hanger next to one of the potted palm-trees; the other one showed the sales room, pyramid and all.

"The reporter even mentioned our desert theme," Ms Gray said happily when she called the inspector in the afternoon. "Our sales have doubled since this morning! Now everyone is **keen on** buying 'Petite Fleur du Jardin' dresses – specially the blue ones. Thank you for making sure that the press presented 'Gray's' so nicely!"

But the man with the special interest in the "Summer Sea" model did not step forward. Perhaps he was on holiday. Perhaps he did not read the papers.

Or perhaps he was the murderer.

Exercise 8: Markieren Sie mit richtig ✔ oder falsch – !

1. The dummy disappeared last year from "Gray's" storage room. ❒
2. The housekeeper puts cinnamon into her hot chocolate. ❒
3. O.U. Gray used to be a successful businessman. ❒
4. Old Mrs Kennedy watered her flowers twice that day. ❒
5. The check-up on Emily Gray's bookkeeping offered new clues. ❒
6. Mrs Gray was not happy about the article in "The Times". ❒

4 Inspector Hudson Receives a Letter

Then Sue Baker's father called to report that his wife had remembered something about a "secret **admirer**" their daughter had mentioned to her.

"A secret admirer?" Hudson asked.

"Yes, sir. My wife is feeling a bit better – of course she isn't over the loss of our daughter yet. But at least she can now accept the fact that Sue is gone," Mr Baker said. "And she just remembered that Sue had said something about a man showing a lot of interest in her."

The inspector was all ears. "Did she say who he was? Did she give a name?"

admirer	Verehrer(in)
necklace	Halskette
to punish	bestrafen

"No, she just said that he was in a difficult position and did not want her to talk about him. She shouldn't tell anyone before he had sorted out his problems. My wife got the impression that he might be married. Sue only mentioned him because her mother found a pearl **necklace** in her room while cleaning it. So she asked Sue where she got those pearls, and after a bit of questioning Sue told her."

"Can your wife remember anything else Sue might have mentioned? Like where she met this man, how long she had known him, things like that?"

Hudson heard Sue's father sigh sadly. "No, Inspector. Believe me, I would tell you if I knew. The murderer of my daughter must be **punished** for what he did to her!"

"Yes, sir," Hudson said with great respect for the grieving father. "I feel the same way."

None of Sue's girlfriends knew anything about a secret admirer. Neither did the two other waitresses at the "Old Lion's Pub".
"A secret admirer who gave her real pearls? How thrilling!" the waitress from Jamaica said. "I wish I had a secret admirer like that, too! Then I'd quit this place in no time! Would you like a glass of 'Pale Ale'? It's our special brand."
The inspector shook his head. "Thank you, but I never drink alcohol while I'm working."
The pretty waitress glanced at Hudson. "What about after you're done working?" she asked sweetly. "It's on the house."
Smiling, Hudson had to decline her offer.
The other waitress, who was from Newcastle and had to work on her day off to replace Sue, shrugged. "If I were you, I'd ask Paul about that secret admirer stuff," she said in a tired voice. "He was keen on her, and he happens to be married. Aren't all secret admirers simply married chaps? Plus he's making a lot of money from this place – not that we see a lot of it, though."

ϟ quit	kündigen; verlassen
brand	Marke, Warenzeichen
decline	ablehnen
offer	Angebot
appraisingly	einschätzend
wall panelling	Wandvertäfelung
distressed	besorgt, beunruhigt

"So Paul is the owner of this pub?" James Hudson inquired. He looked appraisingly at the noble wooden floor and wall panelling. It looked like real cherry wood.
"Yes, Inspector. You can find him in his office. It's right back there, next to the kitchen."
The man who opened the door to his office looked distressed. "Yes?" he asked.

Exercise 9: **Übersetzen Sie die folgenden Sätze!**

1. Did you find the secret admirer you were looking for?

   ____

2. It isn't really a colour at all.

   ____

3. The inspector had a good eye for colours.

   ____

4. He glanced at the tempting scrambled eggs.

   ____

5. Scotland Yard had indeed been waiting for a second letter.

   ____

6. We do exactly what he expects us to do.

   ____

Inspector Hudson introduced himself and **flashed** his badge. "Are you the owner of this pub?" he asked.

"Yes, so what?"

"I understand Sue Baker worked here," Hudson said. "Therefore I must ask you a few questions."

Paul Wynfield frowned. He was about thirty-five and had blue eyes and thick brown hair. He had rough features and a tiger's head tattooed on his upper arm. Bernadine would probably have found him a "good-looking boxer sort of chap", James thought.

"But your men were already here on Monday, asking all kinds of

to flash	*hier:* vorzeigen

ϟ to snoop round	ϟ herumschnüffeln
in charge of	zuständig für
outraged	erzürnt, aufgebracht
said	besagte(r,s)
interrogation	Verhör
stride	Schritt

questions! So why are you **snooping round** here now as well? Didn't I read in the papers about you? Aren't you the chap the Yard always puts **in charge** when a case is hopeless?"
"If you want to put it that way – then I'm the one," Hudson replied calmly.
"So why aren't you out there finding the one who did that to Sue?" Paul Wynfield asked **outraged**.
"That's exactly what I'm doing, sir," Hudson said. "I need to ask you if you might have given her a pearl necklace. Some man she called her 'secret admirer' gave her **said** necklace, and it was more than likely a married man with a high income – like yourself."
Wynfield pushed his chair back and rose. "What is this – an **interrogation**? Are you suspecting me of having killed poor Sue? With a few quick **strides** he walked over to the small window and turned his back on the inspector. "Why on earth should I go and kill Sue? I liked her! Everyone liked her! She couldn't hurt a fly! Why would anybody do something like this to her?"
His voice broke. To the inspector's surprise the tall man with the broad shoulders started to cry. His back still turned on Hudson, he sobbed, "Sue and I – I mean, there was nothing between us – I have a wife and children, you know. But I really liked her a lot – well, yes, I did give her those pearls. I would have liked to give her a lot more, but, oh well –"
He got a hold on himself, wiped his eyes with the back of his hand and turned round. "Inspector," he said **pleadingly**, "you must

pleadingly	flehend, bittend
moreover	darüber hinaus, im Übrigen
to dump	abwerfen, ablegen

believe me! I could never have killed her."

"I want to believe you," Hudson responded. Even though the man had known Sue and might have had a motive to kill her, that still did not explain the murder of the first victim. Unless he happened to have known her, too. But still Hudson had to check if Paul Wynfield had an alibi. It was simple police procedure.

"Just tell me where you were last Sunday night between eleven and three o'clock the following morning. Just so we can eliminate you as a possible suspect."

"At home. Ask my wife," the pub owner answered. "I closed up here and left about eleven fifteen, as usual. Then I drove straight home."

"When did you get home?"

"About half an hour later. Driving home takes about that long."

"And your wife was home? Can she confirm that you arrived home round quarter to twelve?"

Wynfield nodded. "Of course she can confirm that. She was still awake when I got home."

Not the best of alibis, the inspector thought. A wife can confirm anything if she does not want to send her husband off to prison. Moreover, if the pub owner had been quick, he could have given Sue a lift and strangled her inside his car. Then he could have dressed and dumped her body by the river, which was only a few minutes' drive away from the pub. He would still have made it home without losing enough time for anyone to notice.

"Can anyone else confirm your times? Did anyone see you leave the pub or arrive home? Any neighbours?"

Wynfield frowned and shook his head. "No, not that I remember."

Hudson thanked him and left. He was lost in thoughts. The man did not have much of an alibi, but he also did not have much of a motive. Also, there did not seem to by any connection between him and the first woman who had got killed over five weeks ago.
"So, Inspector – did you find the secret admirer you were looking for?" the waitress from Newcastle called after him on his way out. When he turned round, she was wiping down a table, smiling knowingly at him.

to transfer	verbinden

Of course Mrs Wynfield was able to confirm that her husband had come home about eleven forty-five on Sunday night and had not left the house until the next morning at seven.
"What's all this about, anyhow?" she asked upset. "Why should he have anything to do with the murder of one of his waitresses?"
"Just a routine check, Madam," the inspector answered discreetly. After all he did not want to be responsible for the break-up of a marriage.

Exercise 10: Wie heißt das Past Participle der folgenden unregelmäßigen Verben?

1. pay ____________	5. hold ____________
2. lose ____________	6. ring ____________
3. spend ____________	7. know ____________
4. wear ____________	8. tell ____________

Friday afternoon the mysterious stranger who had been so interested in the blue dress rang up Scotland Yard. The call was **transferred** over to Hudson's line.

⚡ bloke	⚡ Typ, Kerl
to offend	beleidigen, kränken

After Hudson had taken down the caller's name and address, he asked the man, "So you are the male customer who was looking at the blue dresses at 'Gray's Boutique' a few months ago?"
"Yes, I think so," the man, whose name was Mr Graham, said nervously. "Even though I have no idea what this is all about. But I did go to 'Gray's' a few months ago to find something for my wife's birthday. And I saw a blue dress I thought she might like. But she is very particular about colours, and so I ended up putting it back. I'm glad I did! She just bought herself an olive blouse at 'Gray's'. I never would have picked that colour for her, but that's my wife!"
"An olive blouse?" the inspector asked. He dimly remembered the woman who had been looking at the rows of blouses when he had stopped by "Gray's" early this week.
"Yes. She calls it olive, but I would say it's a sickly greenish grey" he answered.
"I may have met your wife when I was at the boutique this week," Hudson said astonished.
"That's possible, sir. Usually she ends up buying pink stuff, but when she came home from her last shopping tour, she said one of those blokes from Scotland Yard had walked in. He had had nothing better to do than tell her not to buy that pink blouse she had picked out."
Flustered, Hudson apologized, "I'm sorry if I have offended your wife, Mr Graham. I just thought that pink was a touch too pink. But of course it was none of my business."
"Well, I'm glad you told her, Inspector!" Graham replied. "She actually looks surprisingly good in that olive blouse and is very pleased

with it. She said that inspector from Scotland Yard may have been rude, but that he had a good eye for colours!"

The letter arrived on Saturday. It was addressed to "Scotland Yard, London". There was neither a street address nor a postal code on the envelope.

Hudson's home phone rang the minute he was starting on the breakfast Miss Paddington had prepared for him after letting him **sleep in**. The Yard called him in to take a look at the package bearing "Jack the Skipper's" handwriting. He glanced at the **tempting scrambled eggs** with fried sausages and tomatoes, the steaming toast and the fresh biscuits and sighed. Then he hurried over to his office. The envelope was already waiting for him on his desk.

The inspector took one look at the small package and knew what was inside. The printed letters and the incomplete address told him enough.

to sleep in	ausschlafen
tempting	verlockend, verführerisch
scrambled eggs *pl*	Rührei
tweezers *pl*	Pinzette
to alert	alarmieren

"The arrogance," he murmured while opening it carefully. "The arrogance of not bothering to even write a full address! He considers himself to be too important for that. He knows we were waiting for his second letter and expects us to recognize it immediately –" cautiously he took out a folded sheet with the help of **tweezers**, "– and we do! We do exactly what he expects us to do."

Scotland Yard had indeed been waiting for a second note from "Jack the Skipper", and the secretary who handled all incoming letters had been **alerted** to be on the lookout for an envelope just like this one. So she had sent it on to Inspector Hudson before even opening it.

to choke	ersticken
trace	Beweisspur

He unfolded the piece of paper and read the printed text: "Hello, Inspector Hudson! I heard they put you in charge of my case. If you really are as competent as they say, then why haven't you knocked on my door yet? The second lamb **choked** on this blue belt (just check the marks on her pretty neck if you don't believe me!). The next little lamb won't die in colour – but rather in a bad mood... Love and Kisses, Jack the Skipper."

Sure enough the blue belt that matched the second victim's dress was in the envelope as well. The inspector did not touch it. The crime scene experts had to examine it for **traces** first. If they were lucky, they might get the murderer's fingerprint or some traces from the clothes he had been wearing that night.

Hudson put down the letter and stared at it. How did "Jack the Skipper" know who had been assigned to the case? That fact had not yet been made public. The public did not know. But the murderer did. So what did that mean?

It could only mean one thing: "Jack the Skipper" was either one of the men Hudson had already interviewed, or he had been told by someone that the famous inspector was going round, asking a lot of questions.

Exercise 11: Markieren Sie mit richtig ✔ oder falsch – !

1. Sue told her father about her secret admirer. ❐
2. Paul Wynfield arrived home at ten o'clock that night. ❐
3. Mr Graham is pleased with his wife's olive blouse. ❐

5 Tomatoes and Other Clues

Unfortunately, like the first note and belt, the second note and the blue belt offered no fingerprints. Of course there was plenty of trace evidence on the belt – tiny bits of dirt, plants and sand, traces that matched those found on the dresses. This was to be expected, since the victim had been found outside on the ground. Two single hairs were found on the belt, but they only matched the victim's own long dark hair. The inspector was interested in a tiny fibre, however. He whistled to himself. It was a dark blue cotton-polyester blend and most likely came from a T-shirt. Identical fibres had been found on both dresses. So the sender of the belt had to have been at both crime scenes.

tiny	klein, winzig
fibre	Faser
blend	Mischung
hold up in court	vor Gericht standhalten
shaky	wackelig
pressed for time	unter Zeitdruck

Well, that's a start, he thought. If we find the T-shirt that matches that fibre, then we may have a piece of evidence that will hold up in court.

But first he had to find the person who had been wearing that blue T-shirt.

Inspector Hudson decided to take a closer look at the only two possible suspects he had so far. Both had an alibi, even though Wynfield's was shaky, yet it still was an alibi. But Hudson was pressed for time because "Jack the Skipper" had already mentioned a third victim who "won't die in colour – but rather in a bad mood".

to abandon	aufgeben, verlassen
to bury	begraben, vergraben
bowl	Schale, Schüssel
tasty	lecker

What did he mean by that? And why did he write "in colour"? Did he mean the colour of the dresses he had made them wear? Even though Mrs Graham thought Hudson to have an eye for colours, he did not think of beige as being a real colour.

Monday morning Hudson would have his men check into O.U. Gray's background, and into Paul Wynfield's as well. If it was true that the murderer always struck during full moon, then James Hudson had three more weeks to find him. But for now there wasn't much he could do over the weekend. He wondered if Miss Paddington could warm up that delicious breakfast he had abandoned over an hour ago.

"Of course I can," she said when he got home. "I'll warm up the biscuits and scramble some fresh eggs for you. But then I'll have to hurry off to my painting class."

The inspector followed her into the kitchen.

"Still the 'Rose in Glass'?" he asked. "Or did you have to bury that project?"

Scrambling up two eggs, she said, "The poor rose died on me. But it was too difficult for a first still life, anyhow. Now I'm painting tomatoes instead. They're red and round and rather easy to paint. I'll call the painting 'Tomatoes in Bowl'."

"Sounds tasty," the inspector commented dryly.

The background checks took several days. The first piece of information about O.U. Gray's background came unofficially – and from Elvira Elliot.

"O.U. Gray is the grandson of James Updike, the founder of the Updike Shipyard," she reported to Hudson. "His full name is Oscar Updike Gray. That's because his mother's last name is his middle name. It is said in certain circles that he was supposed to take over the Updike family business, but that he just couldn't manage that. Apparently that was a great disappointment to his grandfather and his mother. His mother doesn't think much of his art, but she is very proud of his twin sister's successful business."

founder	Gründer
apparently	anscheinend
valuable	wertvoll, kostbar
thoroughness	Gründlichkeit

"The Updike Shipyard, you said? That's very interesting," Hudson said, whistling through his teeth. "And you found out all that in such short time? So when are you going to join us here at the Yard? We could use an investigative talent like yours!"

"Never," Elvira answered. But she was smiling. He could hear her smile on the telephone right before she rang off.

So O.U. Gray was connected to a shipyard. Could that be the meaning of "Skipper"? But he had not become a skipper – to the great disappointment of his grandfather and his mother.

Did killing make him feel like less of a disappointment? Like a winner? As if he was in control of his life? As if he was the skipper his family had wanted him to become?

James Hudson had to wait on the results of the two background checks. Two of his character features that made him such a valuable member of Scotland Yard were his thoroughness and his impatience. He simply did not like to sit and wait.

So he decided to find out more about the first victim's past. Could there be any connection between the two victims after all?

Exercise 12: Welches Wort ist das „schwarze Schaf"? Unterstreichen Sie!

1. see sea saw seen
2. smile grin cry laugh
3. jacket trousers coat anorak
4. boys childs girls children
5. eyes feet nose mouth

He rang up Melinda Jordan's former colleagues and friends. He asked a lot of questions about her habits, interests and activities. She had liked the cinema, musicals and reading books. She had loved to travel – mostly to Italy and Spain for her summer holidays. She had enjoyed cooking pasta and dancing salsa. Really **nothing out of the ordinary**. But then he struck gold.

About six years ago Melanie Jordan had worked at the "Pale Ale **Brewery**", a small brewery in the South of London. She had been in charge of the customers' orders. She had quit that job when a larger firm had made her a better-paying job offer as a secretary.

But for two years Melanie had handled all **orders** – **including** those of the "Old Lion's Pub".

nothing out of the ordinary	nichts Außergewöhnliches
brewery	Brauerei
order	Bestellung
including	einschließlich
to deny	abstreiten, bestreiten
barrel	Fass

When Paul Wynfield was shown photos of Melanie Jordan, he **denied** having known her. He said over and over again that he always ordered his **barrels** of "Pale Ale" over the telephone.

to chat	sich unterhalten
to reveal	enthüllen, aufdecken

But his waitress from Newcastle told a different story. "That's not true, but don't tell him I said so, Inspector. I've been working here for ten years – too long, if you ask me. And Paul used to go everywhere in person. Now he's getting lazy, but a few years ago he didn't believe in making phone calls. 'I get the best results if I deal with people directly,' he would always say."
Melanie's former colleagues confirmed what the waitress had said. It used to be Wynfield's habit to come into their office, chat a little with everyone – specially the ladies – and order five or six barrels of ale.
"How well did he know Melanie Jordan?" Inspector Hudson asked the clerk who had had her desk right across from Melanie's desk.
The woman shrugged. "I couldn't tell you that," she said. "I mean Melanie and I weren't close friends or anything like that. When Paul came over, he talked to me and flirted with her. He always paid her a compliment on her dress or her hair or the way she smiled. But I don't know if they ever went out on a date."

The background check on Wynfield revealed that he had been married for twelve years. So he had already been married at the time Melanie Jordan had been working for "Pale Ale". But the inspector was more interested in another detail about the pub owner's past: Before Wynfield had opened his pub, he had had several different jobs, including working as a cook on a ship.
"Uh oh – so he was a sailor," Hudson murmured, whistling through his teeth. "It doesn't look too good for you, Paul. Could you be our 'Skipper' after all?"

O.U. Gray's past, however, only revealed that he was regularly suffering from bouts of depression. There had been a few times when he had got so depressed that he had had to be hospitalized for a few weeks.
Funny – the man seemed so relaxed and easygoing, Hudson thought. Could he be hiding a different personality behind his friendly exterior?
The person who could answer that question best was Miss Paddington. You could not hide anything from her. He decided to take her to "Gray's Boutique" soon to have a look at O. U. G.'s paintings. But a depression does not make a murderer yet, and Paul Wynfield had just become Suspect Number One on the inspector's list. Here was a former connection to a ship, and he had lied about the fact that he had personally known the first victim.

to suffer	(er)leiden
bout	Anfall
to hospitalize	ins Krankenhaus einliefern
exterior	Äußeres
statement	*hier:* Aussage
to confess	gestehen
to avert one's eyes	die Augen abwenden

When the owner of the "Old Lion's Pub" was confronted with the statements made by Melanie's former colleague, he broke down and confessed.
"Yes, yes, I did know her," he confessed. "She used to work at the brewery some years ago. But that doesn't mean that I killed her, does it, Inspector?"
"Then why did you lie to me?" Hudson asked. "Now things look even worse for you."
Wynfield averted his eyes. "I don't know. I read about Melanie's murder in the papers and was shocked. Then – four weeks later –

search warrant	Durchsuchungsbefehl
receipt	Quittung
mere	nur, rein, bloß
to charge with murder	des Mordes anklagen
to scatter	verstreuen
canvas	Leinwand

my own waitress is strangled the same way Melanie was. It's a coincidence, but it makes me look as if I killed them both."

Wynfield gave the same alibi for the night Melanie Jordan was killed – that he had been home with his wife. Of course she confirmed his alibi again. A search warrant of Wynfield's home did not shed any new light on the matter. No dark blue T-shirt was found that might have matched the fibres on the victims' clothes. No receipts from "Gray's" for any dresses bought there.

It could be a mere coincidence that Wynfield had known both women personally and that he had been a sailor in the past. It looked suspicious but it was not enough to charge him with murder.

All Hudson could do was tell Paul Wynfield not to leave the City of London.

And wait for the next murder to happen.

Miss Paddington liked the idea of being hired as a police psychologist – even if it was just for a day.

"But of course I'll go there with you and take a look at the paintings," she declared. She was sitting on the terrace; her painting utensils were scattered everywhere. "Let me just clean up here first."

For the next five minutes she was busy putting away her paints and brushes. When she picked up a white canvas with nothing but two red dots on it, the inspector asked curiously, "Are those two red dots the 'Tomatoes in Bowl'?"

Exercise 13: Lösen Sie das Kreuzworträtsel!

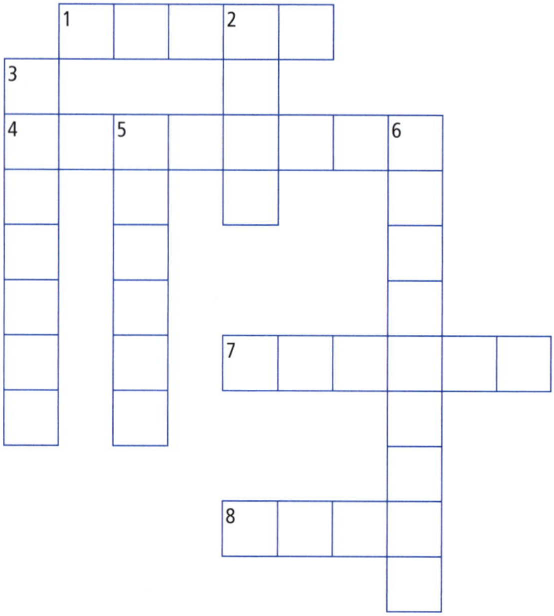

Across

1. Trent got in with a bad one.
4. Something you didn't plan or expect happens by...
7. a deep, narrow valley
8. another word for speed or tempo

Down

2. to force or squeeze something into a small space
3. A house that has a ghost is...
5. When the waves are wild and not calm, the sea is...
6. to be very, very scared

vermilion	Zinnober(rot)
layman	Laie
to bet	wetten
to rush	eilen, rennen, hasten
grey mood	trübe, depressive Stimmung
immortal	unsterblich

"Well, I'm not finished yet. I just started on my first still life," she said a bit offended, adding, "and anyhow – they are not red. That colour is called 'vermilion'."

"They look nice," James Hudson said hastily. "They have a very pretty colour. Actually they look very juicy."

"You think so?" the housekeeper asked happily. "I'll put them into an ultramarine bowl. That's 'blue' for laymen."

"Ultramarine? It sounds like the ocean," Hudson commented.

"It is like the ocean – it is a brilliant sea blue. Look, this is the bowl I will paint." When Miss Paddington brought him a bowl as blue as the dress the second victim had worn, something clicked in Hudson's mind.

"What other names do you professional painters have for colours?" he wanted to know.

"Well, beige is 'ochre' –"

Oh my God, Hudson thought. "O" for ochre and for Oscar – "U" for ultramarine and Updike – and the "bad mood" for – for Gray! O.U. Gray. The colours the victims wore stood for the murderer's initials! And he is planning to kill a third woman. I bet she would have worn a grey dress, Hudson thought, rushing to the phone.

O.U. Gray had played his evil game with Scotland Yard long enough. He had been laughing to himself, dressing his victims in colours that for him, the artist, spelled out his name and his mood: a grey mood was a bout of depression. He who had become a painter instead of a "skipper" wanted to become immortal by killing three women as an "act of art".

compensate	kompensieren
rag	Lumpen
wig	Perücke

"Yes, that is likely." Miss Paddington nodded when Hudson told her his theory of the murderer's motive, after he had telephonically ordered that Gray's flat be searched for certain items. "If he feels like a failure, he will compensate for that by doing something the world will really notice."

But the inspector had already grabbed his car keys to rush to his office.

In O.U. Gray's flat the officers found not only Gray himself, but also a painter's rag which used to be a dark blue T-shirt, a tape recorder with his voice singing a pop song and a dummy, wearing a wig with short dark hair. Through the white curtains it looked like the artist himself was sitting on a chair, painting.

When asked, his sister admitted that her brother had managed the shop for two days in spring, while she had been ill with the flu. That was when he had taken three dresses and rang up the bill, putting the correct amount of money into the cash register.

When Hudson called Elvira Elliot that evening to tell her the good news, she was shocked. "O.U. Gray is the Thames Murderer? I can't believe it! A murderer? Why would he go round and kill women? Why, his new series of three paintings, the 'Moonshine Serenade', was just bought for a lot of money by a New York gallery!"

"The 'Moonshine Serenade'?" the inspector asked.

"Yes, the three pictures at 'Gray's Boutique'. That's the title he gave them. Why do you ask?" Elvira wanted to know.

Now he could tell her. "Because he killed the two women during a full moon. And he announced a third murder – he most likely planned it for the night of the next full moon."

audible	hörbar
to clear one's throat	sich räuspern
gracefully	anmutig

Elvira's shiver was almost **audible**. "Now I don't think I will buy that peachy dress after all," she said. "It would seem like a bad omen."

Hudson had to agree. "Yes," he said and **cleared his throat**. "It's a shame, though. I know you would have looked lovely in that dress – but then you always do, anyway."

"Thank you, James," she said **gracefully** in that sultry voice of hers.

Exercise 14: Beantworten Sie die folgenden Fragen!

1. Why was the inspector so interested in the tiny dark blue fibre?

   ____

2. Why did Miss Paddington decide to paint tomatoes?

   ____

3. Where did Paul Wynfield work as a cook?

   ____

4. Where did the police officers find the dark blue T-shirt?

   ____

5. What had Mrs Graham really seen during the night of the murder?

   ____

Abschlusstest Lösungen

Abschlusstest

Exercise 1: Bilden Sie die richtigen Pluralformen!

1. Peter watched the cat eating a mouse.

   ____

2. Stanley Cooper's henchman was in hospital.

   ____

3. He poured himself another whisky.

   ____

4. Her lifeless body was lying on the cold kitchen floor.

   ____

Exercise 2: Welche Gegenteile gehören zusammen?

1.	☐ innocent	a) neat
2.	☐ jovially	b) doubtful
3.	☐ convinced	c) shabby
4.	☐ posh	d) guilty
5.	☐ littered	e) matter-of-factly

Exercise 3: Verbinden Sie die passenden Ausdrücke!

1.	☐ be up to	a) tears
2.	☐ an inside	b) no good
3.	☐ burst into	c) a grudge
4.	☐ hold	d) job

Exercise 4: Lösen Sie das Kreuzworträtsel!

Across

1. older than a child but not an adult
4. a phone you can carry with you
6. an assistant who works in an office
10. a gentle wind
11. a small house

Down

2. very tired
3. not clean
5. unwanted plants
7. a dead body
8. plants and animals
9. a badger's home

Lösungen

Frightened to Death

Exercise 1: 1. doorbell 2. surprise 3. front 4. neighbours

Exercise 2: 1. Is everything all right? 2. just in case 3. a familiar voice 4. the china plates

Exercise 3: 1. b 2. b 3. a 4. b

Exercise 4: arrived (departed), on the side (in the middle), interested (bored), in front of (behind), afterwards (before), shaking his head (nodding)

Exercise 5: 1. Miss Giles called the ambulance. 2. A man dressed in black who is at least six feet tall. 3. Inspector Davies is thinner than Sergeant Jones. 4. Miss Giles read Catherine's tea leaves.

Exercise 6: 1. d 2. a 3. b 4. c

Exercise 7: 1. accidentally 2. skeleton 3. unlock 4. excited

Exercise 8: 1. are searching 2. works 3. has/had investigated 4. have been reading 5. was reading 6. told

Exercise 9: 1. nodding 2. voice 3. carrying 4. forensics 5. neighbour 6. comfortable 7. kettle

Exercise 10: 1. pansy 2. crowd 3. windowsill 4. injury 5. accuse 6. offend
Lösung: police

Exercise 11: 1. d 2. b 3. a 4. c

Exercise 12:
1. We'll have the letter examined tomorrow.
2. He wanted to keep her company yesterday evening.
3. Shall I put the kettle on now?

Exercise 13: 1. heavily, heaviness 2. suspiciously, suspicion 3. helplessly, helplessness 4. innocently, innocence

Exercise 14: 1. on 2. told 3. could have 4. had said

Exercise 15: 1. sergeant 2. her 3. stairs 4. time

Exercise 16: 1. What 2. How 3. When 4. How

Death in the Woods

Exercise 1: young, rested, full, thick, black, messy, relaxing

Exercise 2: 1. isolated 2. struggle 3. complain 4. undergrowth

Exercise 3: 1. Stephen's boots. 2. The caller's name. 3. Stephen's mother's voice. 4. The two constables' torches. 5. George Morris' family.

Exercise 4: 1. falsch 2. richtig 3. falsch 4. richtig

Exercise 5: 1. was listening 2. was holding 3. looked 4. felt 5. was 6. had introduced

Exercise 6: 1. exchanged 2. was 3. called 4. didn't 5. looked

Exercise 7: 1. a 2. b 3. b 4. a

Exercise 8: 1. hear 2. sympathetic 3. witness 4. calm 5. chaotic 6. full

Exercise 9: 1. woods 2. silently 3. cottage 4. stepson 5. policeman 6. superior 7. shook **Lösung:** witness

Exercise 10: 1. in 2. from 3. out 4. of 5. at 6. in

Exercise 11: 1. violent 2. stupid 3. sunrise 4. frantic 5. courage 6. impatience

Exercise 12: 1. stopped 2. went 3. shouted 4. came 5. demanded

Exercise 13: 1. The police arrested Stephen first. 2. Arthur told his wife he was going to hunt rabbits. 3. Arthur thought George owed him money. 4. Arthur's wife told the police he was not at home when George was murdered.

Exercise 14: 1. paler 2. close, closest 3. gentle, gentler 4. worse, worst 5. quiet, quietest 6. formal, most formal 7. more confident, most confident

Exercise 15: 1. gently 2. nervously 3. earnestly 4. miserably 5. comfortingly

Exercise 16: 1. c 2. d 3. a 4. b

Exercise 17: 1. went 2. didn't 3. leave 4. in 5. there 6. would 7. Did 8. who

Dressed to Die

Exercise 1: 1. Suddenly Jennifer heard a faint bark behind her. 2. The wet something looked like a mop of black hair. 3. He almost overlooked an old woman crossing the street. 4. The murder case would be reported in today's newspaper. 5. Her old parents lived in a village. 6. The dresses were the connection he had been looking for.

Exercise 2: 1. decade 2. scrub 3. belt 4. whistle 5. victim

Exercise 3: 1. She was looking forward to her holiday with her husband. 2. He had sent a note and a beige belt. 3. Miss Paddington burned her pork pie because she hadn't slept all night. 4. Both women were strangled with a belt. 5. Only her cat Lizzy noticed her absence.

Exercise 4: 1. Er betrat eine andere Welt. 2. Die Frau sah, dass er ihren Einkauf betrachtete. 3. Ihre Gesichtszüge waren etwas hart. 4. Ich zeigte ihm das Kleid in allen Farben. 5. Der Kunde schien vor allem an dem blauen Kleid interessiert zu sein.

Exercise 5: 1. will 2. is going to 3. will 4. will 5. going 6. going 7. is going to

Exercise 6: 1. The heat wave was finally replaced by rain. 2. The dresses were attractively displayed inside the shop. 3. The inspector didn't come here to discuss the artwork. 4. Gray poured himself a glass of freshly made lemonade. 5. She is an old lady living by herself. 6. Perhaps he did not read the papers.

Exercise 7: 1. garment/dress 2. rose/blossom 3. jug/glass 4. irritated/upset 5. liquid/ lemonade 6. accessories/belt 7. afford/expensive

Exercise 8: 1. falsch 2. richtig 3. falsch 4. richtig 5. falsch 6. falsch

Exercise 9: 1. Haben Sie den heimlichen Verehrer gefunden, den Sie gesucht haben? 2. Es ist eigentlich gar keine Farbe. 3. Der Inspektor hatte ein gutes Auge für Farben. 4. Er warf einen Blick auf die verlockenden Rühreier. 5. Scotland Yard hatte tatsächlich auf einen zweiten Brief gewartet. 6. Wir tun genau das, was er von uns erwartet.

Exercise 10: 1. paid 2. lost 3. spent 4. worn 5. held 6. rung 7. known 8. told

Exercise 11: 1. falsch 2. falsch 3. richtig

Exercise 12: 1. sea 2. cry 3. trousers 4. childs 5. feet

Exercise 13: 1. crowd 2. wedge 3. haunted 4. accident 5. choppy 6. terrified 7. ravine 8. pace

Exercise 14: 1. It was a piece of evidence that would hold up in court. 2. They were easy to paint. 3. He had worked on a ship. 4. They found it inside O.U. Gray's flat. 5. She had seen the dummy dressed up like the artist.

Abschlusstest

Exercise 1: 1. Peter watched the cats eating mice. 2. Stanley Cooper's henchmen were in hospital. 3. They poured themselves another whisky. 4. Their lifeless bodies were lying on the cold kitchen floor.

Exercise 2: 1. d 2. e 3. b 4. c 5. a

Exercise 3: 1. b 2. d 3. a 4. c

Exercise 4: 1. teenager 2. exhausted 3. dirty 4. mobile 5. weeds 6. secretary 7. corpse 8. nature 9. sett 10. breeze 11. cottage